Frank Richard Faller was born in Scotland. A graduate of Glasgow University, he continued his education in English Literature, Communication and Law in Canada. He has also completed postgraduate work in educational research. His career background includes the Civil Service, aviation, the oil and energy industries and management consulting.

He has researched and implemented practical ways of assessing self-determination, and improving attitudes to both work and social situations. His central interests lie in clear communication, orderly approaches to decision-making and personal growth through openness of mind. He provides consulting and training services to various business sectors and organizations.

RE-CREATE YOURSELF

Positive Strategies for Self-Development

Frank Richard Faller

Thorsons
An Imprint of HarperCollins*Publishers*

Thorsons
An Imprint of HarperCollins*Publishers*
77–85 Fulham Palace Road,
Hammersmith, London W6 8JB

Published by Thorsons 1992
10 9 8 7 6 5 4 3 2 1

A catalogue record for this book
is available from the British Library

ISBN 0 7225 2558 3

Printed in Great Britain by
HarperCollinsManufacturing Glasgow

Contents

Part 4: What is Missing? Are you Ready for Success?

Preface

So you want to organize yourself to achieve more with your life? I know the feeling! I'll be candid with you: self-improvement is not something that has come easily to me. When I encountered life's inevitable crossroads, I examined my set of dog-eared life-maps many times. It took courage to admit that my current and desired positions were not the same point. Acting on this realization was hardest of all. When we come to that crossroads, we need help. I want to give you a head start on your journey.

The principles of self-improvement have been well established through modern psychology and positive thinking. But this book takes you beyond theories and rousing words. It *compels you to search within yourself, plan and act!* Quite simply, it offers thoughtful guidance in setting and achieving the *right goals for you*, with emphasis on the enabling power of the focused mind.

Is success a marvellous home or a motor cruiser, a closer relationship with a partner or a parent, control over self-confessed arrogance or rescuing oneself from despair? The notion of a successful and happy life has many connotations, and the prospect of achieving *chosen* success is exciting. In this respect, we could all do better! Yet goal-setting makes some of us uncomfortable. By limiting ourselves with reservations, we stifle the magnificent potential within us. However, if we determine what we truly want, life is *not* limited, but full of purpose, wonder and promise. My theme is plain but elegant: *Avoid living life by default! Live the good life by conscious choice!*

This book helps to redraw your dusty old maps, and select the right bearings. I hope you will find my approach fresh, challenging, humorous and helpfully provocative. There are no intellectual mountains to be crossed, but prepare yourself for discovery nonetheless.

Frank Richard Faller

Acknowledgements

There are many contributors to a book of this type, and so many who do not realize where they have contributed. Many of the themes and ideas have developed through several years of professional association with people from all walks of life, in all possible situations. Specifically, situational focus was provided by working environments and the people who played their parts. Various training, consulting, counselling and group sessions around the world have given otherwise academic material a practical dimension. To the individuals involved, I offer my gratitude.

Special acknowledgements are due to family members and friends who have discussed various issues in self-improvement before and during writing. In particular, I am indebted to the input and encouragement from Susan Cawley and RSA Symons (UK), and the appreciation of constructive human attitudes from the late Tom Stevenson of Washington State, USA.

PART 1
Where Are You Right Now?

FORWARD PASSAGE...
FROM NEGATIVE...

TO POSITIVE

'I've so many things on, I can't think straight.'

'Self-help books usually give me a lift if they're any good, but that's as far as I ever get.'

'My bed was made long ago; now I must lie in it. Changing things now would be impossible.'

'People know me as I am. Isn't that my natural self?'

'Some people like me, some don't. I'm the same with them. It seems to work.'

'Focusing on the things which matter will put my energies where I want them.'

'Learning has a purpose and I intend to apply what I learn.'

'I alone decide what comes next; change is always an option.'

'My growth will involve change: no law says I must stand still.'

'Mastering interpersonal skills is a key part of my self-development.'

1 Standing at the Crossroads

The person who risks nothing, does nothing, has nothing, is nothing, and becomes nothing. He may avoid suffering and sorrow, but he simply cannot learn and feel and change and grow and love and live. He has forfeited his freedom. Only the person who risks is truly free.

Anonymous

OVERVIEW
If we cannot be clear on what we want from life, how can we possibly grumble when nothing is achieved? By taking charge of our lives, we can choose our future. Standing at the crossroads, our decision point, we have three choices: apathy (standing still), drifting (the easy path) and conscious future (our path).
Self-improvement is a personal quest. We must choose the right goals to aim for. This invites change into our lives. But life is magnificent once we risk a little, and understand the secrets!

WHAT DO YOU WANT?

A dream house? Your own aircraft? Improved relationships? Solutions to problems, frustrations, less anxiety about the future? Your own business perhaps? The offer sounds pretentious, doesn't it? Nevertheless, this book will help you discover exciting possibilities for your life that you've probably never considered. And if the above goals are not exactly what you want, you will learn how to develop some that are.

We have been told by the information age gurus that the future belongs to things of the mind. I would propose that *your future* belongs to things of *your mind*. 'Open' thinking allows us to determine what we really want from life – possessions, personal qualities, a new outlook. You do have control over cause and effect, *but only if you take the first step!* Identifying our life possibilities is difficult, but with some guidance the future can open up beautifully...

STANDING AT THE CROSSROADS

Nothing pleases us more than to believe we are living life as we should! If we can at least experience this feeling during good episodes of our lives, we argue that life is not too unfair. This is a reasonable view of things. Unfortunately, it is difficult to maintain when we have a prolonged setback, or we begin to question our motives, methods and results. Am I achieving enough? Is this all? Where to now? Then we arrive at the crossroads of life, usually without warning or preparation; perhaps we will find ourselves there more than once in our lives. There doesn't have to be an actual crisis to bring us there – sometimes we just feel a need to grow, to explore new dimensions of ourselves, or simply stretch our achievement boundaries. We are active creatures and standing still can be unsettling. The common denominators of the experience are a sense of anxiety and possibly impatience. How do you feel?

FACING UP TO THE ISSUES

The quick and easy solution to all this is to subdue our doubts, ambitions and dreams. That is a certain way to disaster, however. We are human; we are dynamic entities. Life is a gift to be used, all the way out to its edges and beyond. In fact we are usually interested in acquiring knowledge and skills; we spend years learning them. But we seem reluctant to apply the same level of effort and commitment to our life plan.

In search of new ideas, some fortunate people are sent on personal development seminars by their well-meaning employers. Interpersonal skills, negotiating, conflict management and innovative thinking are likely topics of study. They enhance our intellectual skills – but may do surprisingly little for us when we feel alone at that crossroads. Besides work-sponsored training, people may browse around book-shops for material which will somehow improve their lives. Career counsellors, newspaper horoscopes and personal-column prophets are also consulted. Some people are natural browsers and dabblers. Are you? By studying this book I know you are facing up to the issues of self-improvement. But everyone needs *focus* and guidance.

YOU'RE ON A QUEST

Regardless of the methods, thinking people (that includes you!) are constantly on a quest. There are many quests, but the best are always concerned with human purpose and growth. Have your employers ever asked the question 'Where would you like to be in five years' time?' (Did they know where they would be?) It sounds like a typical staff appraisal question, but my, isn't it disturbing! You might take a few moments to contemplate the significance of forward planning. We defer planning and deal with immediate demands, don't we? But without a plan, we can't exactly go anywhere...can we?

This quest will not take you further than your desk or the kitchen table. It will not lead you to holy men in Nepal. It *will*, however, help you to examine yourself more closely than before. Then you can move on to the practical business of deciding *what you want* in your life, and *how you can bring that about*. The quest aims to help you realize, with joy rather than shock or despair, that you are *not* all you could be. I invite you to deal with a serious subject: YOU!

RIGHT JOURNEY, RIGHT GOALS

You are now setting out on a journey of exploration. Don't worry if you haven't got a complete map. Your next steps will become clear as you move along the road. To make it easier for you, don't take any luggage. (That too will be handled.) No need to worry about being spotted by your friends and associates either. You are alone, but in a vast new crowd of friends and associates, all searching just as you are. The journey is not without risk, for you will uncover apathy, laziness, self-doubt and fear. All human growth inflicts a measure of pain, but rarely do trophies fall into our laps merely by waiting for them.

Life is not a neat set of isolated compartments. People love to think so, but good old change shakes that belief! Rigid ideas, such as celebrating affluence as the only worthwhile goal of the human race, must also face the acid test. If your only aim in life is to get so rich that all other problems can be dealt with (somehow), then be prepared for a tumble at some point. Even the most dedicated high flier must operate among people. Should your goals run rough-shod over your best helpers, then you are going to crash. The objective is to arrive at your destination with much more than material achievements.

A LOOK AT THE MAP FIRST

This book introduces material in progressive lessons, organized to lead you through the essential stages of self-assessment and discussion. There are four parts, each one presenting a topic question.

PART 1: WHERE ARE YOU RIGHT NOW?
(Chapters 1 to 5)

This part will help you take stock of your present position, and become more aware of yourself as a person, assessing your personal qualitites, financial situation and shortfalls.

PART 2: WHERE DO YOU WANT TO BE, IN SPITE OF EVERYTHING?
(Chapters 6 and 7)

We begin by looking ahead to your possible future, determining what you want from life, how to go about making the right choices and confronting negative attitudes created by conditioning.

PART 3: WHAT ARE YOUR GOALS, AND HOW WILL YOU ACHIEVE THEM?
(Chapters 8, 9, 10 and 11)

The process of setting realistic life goals, both personal and material, is explained, together with how to deal with change, understand the nature of stress, and uncover the way to achieve your goals.

PART 4: WHAT IS MISSING? ARE YOU READY FOR SUCCESS?
(Chapters 12, 13 and 14)

Part 4 is concerned with the review and consolidation of ideas. Certain themes are substantiated, and there is a final call to commitment to follow through the plan outlined in the book and achieve success.

YOU ARE ON YOUR WAY

There must be more than you allowed yourself in the past. This programme will build your confidence and develop the courage to *achieve*, to *re-create yourself*. It will reveal the potential magnificence of life once its secrets are understood. You are on your way.

REVIEW

1 You have asked yourself the basic question: *What do I want, and how can I achieve it?*

2 You have been faced with a basic choice: *Which path should I take?*

2 The Open Person

In lateral thinking one is not so concerned with the nature of an arrangement of information but with where it can lead one.

Edward de Bono

OVERVIEW

We are free to make choices, to *create* our lives as we wish. All too often we are limited by fixed approaches, vain illusions and closed thinking. Vague fears keep us from reaching our true potential. An open mind opens up possibilities we ignored previously.

Openness also allows us to tackle painful issues in our lives which we may have suppressed. A positive outlook can only be gained through acceptance rather than denial. The prerequisite condition for changing our lives is to become an Open Person.

WHY IT IS VITAL TO BE OPEN

If you want to achieve anything with your life, start by being honest with yourself. Open up channels within yourself which help you put all things into healthy perspective. It is difficult to be completely open with others, but why not be open with yourself? This means being honest about issues. Neither deny aspects of your behaviour nor sidestep developments which need attention. Accept life gladly, as it happens. Accept the past, but experience today. If the present is unpleasant for you, try and learn from the experience of it right now, and then, when the time comes, move on to something better. If your outlook is open, life will flow along nicely without blockages.

Let's have an example. Perhaps you feel that your career prospects would be greatly improved by taking further education. However, the negatives (finances, family upheaval, unwilling brain cells) cloud the issue. There are two stages of blocking. First (external): your family and friends learn nothing about your career ambitions and feelings about education. Second (internal): you *suppress* the issue *within yourself*. But the education possibility certainly does not go away — it floats up in consciousness several times a day. So nothing is resolved. By not opening up an internal dialogue, good ideas never see the light of day. And that's not going to help you. Self-honesty removes blockages — and you will learn how.

To begin with, regardless of what you may have been told, you are indeed a free person! The expectations set upon you by others are really not as pervasive as you might think. Your own fundamental truths and philosophies of life are not cast in stone; they are simply suppositions real to you for the moment. Begin to understand that flexibility is a key asset. By re-establishing yourself as an independent person and being able to stand apart and think for yourself, you will learn how to *achieve*.

We often allow our freedom to become compromised with nothing substantial in return. Be yourself and believe in yourself! Who said that your life must go on precisely as it does at present? If you are completely fulfilled and want nothing more, then be happy. If that is not the case, be happy in the fact that there *are* alternatives for you — bright, exciting alternatives.

My challenge in writing this book lies in capturing the attention and imagination of your mind. We are naturally suspicious of any outsider attempting to get inside our minds; we have so many secrets and dark corners in there! So, to impress your mind, I must make a string of convincing arguments. Language is the primary tool we have here — yes, it's formal, distant and perhaps inadequate, but the message will triumph over the words! Negatives aside, let us now try to make a fair attempt at establishing what openness is all about.

If you are going to grow as a person, whether you intend to be a tycoon or a saint, you have to be open to life, and to revising your interpretation of it. What would you say if you were told there was nothing wrong with the world, and nothing right with it either? The statement is senseless? Surrealism is for the birds? Well, I admit there is no simple answer. At least, not for the Open Person. But being open is a beginning.

Before you even start to grow into an Open Person, however, your mind needs to know that *something is different* with you these days. Tell your mind that you require a bit of consideration for a change, that you need more flexibility instead of fixed suppositions. Go on, try it.

HOW OPEN MUST WE BE?

Being open means being willing to contemplate and try new approaches. For want of a better philosophy, 'What is there to lose?' works very well. Then there is a *real chance of growth* for you, without dark unknowns spoiling your early enthusiasm. Any fears you may have are usually manageable. For example, suspicion of others 'using information against me' bothers many people. We fear that by opening up just once to other people, they will tell everyone we're over the edge! Opening up in many situations may lead to vulnerability, to another person's advantage, to our getting hurt... Generally, these fears are out of proportion and damaging to our self-identity. Removing fear is part of our task. Without fear, you will have a clearer perspective. You will be able to approach problems and issues with a sense of purpose, and make sound decisions.

At the other extreme, over-indulging in gregariousness (because you've *changed*) is not appropriate either. Some assertiveness training courses turn retiring folks into insufferable loud-mouths! Making an outright fool of yourself is generally not socially acceptable, especially in certain communities or groups. There are set times and places for deviant behaviour. For example, it might be acceptable (and forgiveable) for otherwise conformist women at their office party to grab the male stripper and discover he blushes. But even then, there is always an element of self-consciousness and personal insecurity behind the things we will or will not do, and where and when we do them.

It's a thin line between *holding back* and *being bold*, even if it is sometimes fun to transgress. To overstep boundaries foolishly, however, can invite criticism. In some settings, too much openness is viewed as aggression, disturbing people rather unpleasantly. In a social setting, the rules are usually clear enough. But can you see the parallel between socially balanced behaviour and being open with yourself, deciding *how far* you will go?

Do you find that you conceal this book from your partner, your friends, your boss? Does the subject-matter cause you to be slightly embarrassed? Is it a piece of evidence that you are perhaps less than you should be and you're trying to catch up? Leave a cookbook on the sofa and you'll get no reaction. Leave this book there and welcome your chance to be open! How will you explain yourself? After your feelings of discomfort are out of the way, tell anyone who asks that you want to change yourself by being open to all possibilities. You might discover that as an Open Person you must be open enough to suffer incredulous friends who stereotype you as someone who really does need help! We all really do need help, though, so never think you are trailing behind.

TO BE OPEN IS TO BE HUMAN

To be human, we do share sensitive self-knowledge at times, at least with family or trusted friends. To become open, we need to overcome fear of rejection, fear of criticism, fear of losing self-balance. Strong identification with peer groups or role models may have to be dismantled, or they will keep us as we are. Break out of fearfulness and the power of other people! Discover your own strength and be prepared to accept and love yourself without seeking approval from others. Perhaps you are not perfect, but then, to be open with you, neither am I!

We can all appreciate our own inadequacies while *celebrating* our real potential. Discover again what it really means to be honest. Honesty is a human problem, sometimes an uncomfortable hang-up. When do we know we are completely honest with ourselves? How do we *really* know how we feel? Are our opinions or world view honest enough to rely on?

You might notice it easier to be honest with other people than with yourself, because you know if you are lying to others. This is an area to contemplate and work at. For our present purposes, try not to lie to others, and do try to be honest with yourself! You will become your own best friend in thought and deed.

BE OPEN WITH YOURSELF

Take a notebook right now and make a quick list of the personal faults you know cause you problems. Here's a list of prompts to get you started:

> I moan and whine a lot.
> I get frustrated with tedious people or situations.
> I'm sometimes sarcastic and sharp with people.
> I can be self-centred and selfish at times.
> I look back with sourness on life's problems and setbacks.

Quite a revealing exercise, isn't it? Yes, it concentrates on the negative, but you will learn how to turn the tables and *seek the positive*. Jump right in and learn how to be open with yourself! Now, if you were a fully-grown Open Person, you would feel able to put your list on the wall at work, give your partner one, pin one to the squash club notice board, and place it as a personal advertisement in your local newspaper. Of course, I don't expect you to do this *yet*. For now, I'm satisfied if you recognize your faults, declare them to yourself, and look forward to better things.

DO YOU HAVE A CHIP ON YOUR SHOULDER?

Try some sensitive hang-ups you probably have on material wealth and ambition. Keep the openness flowing. Again, some quick prompts:

> I'll never clear my mortgage this side of the grave.
> My family were always losers.
> Two years of unemployment has fixed me for good.
> It's wrong to want more than you have; it's greedy.
> I just seem to suit a rut – well, it's predictable.

These are typical admissions that we would rather keep close counsel on. We might present ourselves as ambitious, confident and well-adjusted individuals to the outside world, but inside we might be snivelling, self-persecuting defeatists waiting to be hit by the proverbial bus. *Do you want to clear your mortgage?* Be honest, wouldn't you like a new car? What about a new career that truly satisfies you? To make any progress, come clean about the very things that cause you pain: frustration over mortgages, cars, careers... Write them down and see them looking up at you – that tends to dull their power over you. So many people soldier on, carrying albatrosses about with them, saying, 'I'm a failure, so don't keep nagging at me! I can prove to you I can't do any better!' No need for you to be one of them!

DO YOU HAVE FIXED ATTITUDES AND APPROACHES TO THINGS?

We usually find lazy ways of dealing with our everyday events and challenges, whether they are demanding or trivial. A car stalls ahead of us. Do we move around it, sit there blasting the horn, or accept the situation and wait till it starts? Or get out and help? The least trouble-

some course usually wins for the vast majority of people. We have a
sad lack of basic comprehension and initiative when it comes to external situations, and few spontaneous mechanisms to handle them.
Becoming involved is seldom an option: we consume energy justifying
our inaction rather than taking action. It is the projection of this everyday behaviour into our own lives that causes personal growth suffoca-
tion. In the context of your life, you cannot rely on the other person to
pick up the pieces. You have to make the first move. But you are quite
capable of taking the initiative, of taking charge.

So, are you going to consider changing these fixed attitudes and
approaches? If you can break out of rigid patterns imposed by school-
ing, conditioning or just plain habit, you will see the world differently.
In order to see beyond the ordinary and the mundane, to see exciting
possibilities for your life, you have to discard inhibiting patterns of
thought and behaviour. Be open to other ways of looking at things.
Accept that your current view might be valid, but not exhaustive or
unchanging. You may call it 'curiosity' or 'flexibility'. I call it 'being an
Open Person'.

WHAT DOES OPENNESS MEAN TO YOU?

Certain accepted stimuli can be effective in helping us to become more
open. For example, music allows us to relax some inhibitions. We can
join in to some extent, humming, whistling, moving our hands to an
imaginary orchestra or playing a make-believe guitar at a fantasy rock
concert. The Arts help us as far as we want to go. Theatre commands
our sense of abandon with artistic licence: it is socially acceptable, for
example, to explain why Beckett's *Waiting For Godot* holds special
insights for us. We applaud the absurd themes of the play, but deny
our fear of the absurdities in real life. Similarly, love of nature and the
outdoors is considered safe as a conversation piece, providing we
don't get too militant about saving whales or scream incessantly about
acid rain. We allow *conditional* openness, but it's a start.

These accepted stimuli and topics are quite tame: they allow us to
sample and discuss life without confronting burning personal issues.
The action of the stage or a painter's creativity remains at a safe distance, and so we readily tolerate unusual people, ambiguities and
absurd possibilities in a play or a painting. But to remain open to
absurd, sensitive or unusual things *in our everyday lives* is quite different!
We deal with our own ambiguities or hang-ups by keeping them deep
within ourselves, or 'in the family'. And meeting the same distressing

or undesirable things in others is decidedly uncomfortable. Sometimes we experience bad behaviour in another which really disturbs us. What might be happening is a 'reflection reaction', that is, the very thing you dislike about the other person is really the trait you dislike in yourself! Seeing it in another makes you uneasy, angry, but the painful fact is that you are uneasy and angry about that dark corner of yourself. Yet by understanding this type of thing, you can rebuild yourself. Yes, it takes a strong will to change, but the results are worth it. I will help you to light up those dark corners and open up your life!

PATTERNS AND VALUES

We may take great pride in declaring ourselves to be open-minded; this is wrongly analogous to saying we are modern in outlook. So many old established customs and social attitudes have altered in our own lifetime. Consider the changes in divorce law, religious convictions, treatment of the mentally ill and sexual freedom. It is inevitable that these and other human attitudes will keep changing.

People of the older generation feel comfortable with the values and patterns they chose to live by. As new ways appear, in many instances they find them strange, threatening and destructive. The development of collective and individual consciousness in the sixties was viewed by some as a breakthrough, for example, by others as the downward slide of western civilization. The seventies provided a period of retraction, a consolidation of the me mentality. This return to a nominally stable, conservative world view, a move to accepting responsibility rather than rejecting it, was seen by many as a return to sanity. Hence the emergence of politics of 'tried-and-tested common sense', and the 'total management' approach rather than pursuing rigid ideologies. Attitudes in the eighties were different again. Perhaps we will not be able to pass judgement on them until the twenty-first century is well under way.

It is clear, however, that our personal consciousness (and degree of openness) grows up around concurrent states of safety and fear, whatever generation, political ideology or world view we like to associate with. How open can our thinking be against the backdrop of 'society'?

Whenever we associate with a given pattern, a set of values or a consciousness we feel safe with, there are two significant poles to consider. First: the comforting reality of feeling at home with patterns that give life some form. Second: the problems of shifting to an opposing or 'new, untried, ambiguous, threatening' pattern. Both poles are in tension, of course. If we are firm 'believers' in Position A, how can we feel comfortable with Position B? This is where dichotomy is born, a watershed of essential but awkward division in our very process of thinking, the dilemma of free will. You might not be aware of it, but you have tremendous power because of free will. Just think of the choices you could make. You might choose to stop reading this book, make some tea or coffee, meet a friend and so on. Shopping offers many choices. And politics. Religion. Education. Careers. Culture. Music. Relationships. Thinking. The last one is important: it gives infinite choices, not just Position A or B. Quite an encouraging thought, isn't it? Thoughts, choices, possibilities...under your control!

CHALLENGE YOUR TRUSTED PATTERNS

So how can there possibly be such a reality as 'Open Thinking' or 'Open People'? We seem to be tied in knots by our own special selection of patterns and attitudes. To be an Open Person, be willing to set aside your trusted patterns of thought and behaviour. That does not mean you are going to become a dissident of some sort, nor that you will float about agreeing with everyone and everything. The Open Person is one who makes a conscious decision to embrace the other person's view, without necessarily agreeing with it. Bigots just won't succeed in this exercise, nor will fanatics of any calling. But flat-Earth enthusiasts should do very well, if they can just accept that the world might be spherical for a day now and then!

As you move through an average day, people and situations will present themselves to you. Whether you think they are significant or not, become aware of your own thoughts, every hour, every moment. Try this for a whole day, attempting to keep 'open' to every single piece of experience which comes your way. How many times did you have difficulties with basic communication and behaviour arising from other people or situations? Did you have to remind yourself you were being 'open' that day, as we agreed? Not all days turn up illuminating manifestations in Truth, but if you're open enough, you might be surprised at what does come along.

There was a new notice on the bulletin board. It was quite long, professionally done on yellow paper, with striking artwork and typeset letters. James glanced briefly at the heading:

ROCKIN' ALL OVER THE WORLD

He had talked to Adrian twice before about his use of the company's graphic supplies for 'government' jobs. This time he had gone too far. The notice was worth more than some work for clients. It was clear he was just trying this one on, making his point against James' recent promotion to supervisor. He was a popular fellow, reasonably good at his job, but becoming a real prima donna.

On the way to the art department, James met the receptionist, Anne. They nodded as they passed; then James stopped.

'Oh, Anne, could I have a word?'

'Certainly.'

'Have you seen Adrian's notice?'

'Ah, yes, it's good, isn't it?'

Without much more than a 'Hhrrmph!', James proceeded to arty little Adrian's world of paints and sticky papers. He found Adrian leaning over his table.

'This notice on the board, what's wrong with your memory? Or are you half deaf? You arty types, you're all the same! I remember art students at college, they were hippies all right! All show and no responsibility! Well, I'm afraid this...'

Adrian calmly reached to a pile of loose papers. He handed James one sheet, yellow. He glanced down and began to read.

ROCKIN' ALL OVER THE WORLD

Your favourite band (and mine) are still alive
   and appearing at Wembley
   !!! STATUS QUO !!!
   In the company of
   BOB GELDOF AND FRIENDS
   At the occasion of
   RELIEVING SUFFERING
   Among wonderful people on this very Earth
   That were forgotten as a result of
   OUR CLOSED MINDS
   But we have remembered
   OUR COMPASSION, OUR LOVE AND OUR CASH
   Contact Adrian
   Art Department

Work pressures are particularly effective at keeping us from being open. Imagine engineers, scientists or undertakers being totally open in their professions! Managers and supervisors in any work environment feel they must keep that essential distancing phenomenon alive and active. Become too familiar and divulge your little idiosyncrasies at your peril! You may be faced with accusations of weakness, a hierarchal plot against you, or daily snubs from the very staff you confided in. They do love you, but very conditionally... Is it really like this? Well, *only if we allow it!* The Open Person must learn how to live in this real world, but remain true to inner convictions.

TRUTH IS BEING TRUE TO YOURSELF

The secret of being true to yourself is to deal honestly with the dichotomy between what is and what you are *becoming*. People may not give a hoot about your developing inner mind or your secret desire to become a world-class jockey! But don't allow their indifference to limit you in any way. You are in control, and *free to exercise that control*. That is your truth.

What can you do to further this promising cause of being true to yourself and exercising control? Well, when you go about your affairs, try to keep an open mind on developments which are completely unplanned and out of the blue. You might miss something vitally important if you shut your mind to unexpected events. We never know what's around the next corner. It might be the very clue, referral, stimulus or source of innovation you've been waiting for! Here are a few ideas:

- Don't routinely criticize the latest taste in music. Play a few albums and take it all in. See what is real there, for other people.
- If you fancy an outfit in a store sale, but it's just *not* the type of thing people normally see you wearing, buy it, wear it and enjoy it! Your personality might receive a welcome nudge towards poise and freshness.
- When you meet two guests at a party discussing Tarot cards and astrology, ask them what they think about it all, even if you feel that it's myth and nonsense. You might get a free reading with startling insights!
- If you go to a library, force yourself to take books from shelves you've never explored before. New sources mean new ideas.

Do men with ear-rings get to you? How about blue lipstick? Loud clothes? White shoes? Do you feel inadequate around senior executives? Are you having problems accepting different races, religions or sexual preferences? Do teenagers leave you cold and feeling you can't understand them? Are you ignoring and avoiding certain people for some peculiar reason you hold dear? I once taught creative writing to old people. Once the inevitable poems about flowers and falling leaves were exhausted, they wanted *consciousness-raising sessions*. Topics were unlimited and discussions lively. The age factor disappeared. My intellect was humbled and my opinions on age dismantled. That's what happens when you lower your guard! No need to walk in others' shoes, but listen to them for a change. Their view might be just as valid as yours: it may actually expand some of your limited perspectives. Then you can be true to yourself; no illusions, no vanity.

STIMULATION THROUGH VARIETY

Are you snagged in a daily routine? Change it! Take the bus sometimes instead of the car. Take a taxi just for a treat. Try walking. Do you eat 'meat-and-two-veg' because that's what your mother fed you 40 years ago? Eat chili or tacos or lasagne! Are you fed up doing the work you've done for 20 years? Then open up your mind to what else you might be able to do. You make your own rules; why should it be otherwise?

Whenever people went wild about a film, a play, or a show, for example, Justin consciously downgraded and avoided it. Popular entertainment is so much hype, he thought. *Cats* was a prime example. But when he lived in London, the pressure was on to see the musical, so, reluctantly, he bought tickets.

Sitting near the stage, it was impossible to avoid cats. They were everywhere. Smiling, purring, singing cats! Despite his early prejudice, Justin was overcome by the action, lighting, incessant energy, the emotion and magic. It was tremendous! Justin decided it was not just another musical; it was a spiritual experience.

Sometimes we are given so much, are lifted so high, by the least obvious surprises. It takes so little effort to open up positively to things we have prejudged. Yet we resist, alas.

The Open Person recognizes personal shortcomings, but plans to change them. The Open Person tolerates shortcomings in others, and sees opportunities in all things. Fixed ideas, fixed routines, fixed judgements on everything limit you and narrowly define the possibilities of your life. Why do you allow such control over *you*? Are you terrified of living your life to its ultimate potential? If you are going to be on the journey, then take your blinkers off and look at the scenery! It may show you vistas you missed all along.

A friend insisted Julia should go to the wrestling. The very idea insulted her intelligence! 'It's all a put-up,' she said. 'The bouts are all rigged, it's ridiculous anyway; you know the sort of thing.' She knew they would get sick of it after one or two Saturday nights. So on this basis she went, without any enthusiasm whatsoever.

It was another world. Like gladiators, some of them. They took it all so seriously, especially the spectators! Women were the ones to watch: they went berserk if their darling boy was getting cabbage ears from a bully. The action eclipsed the futility of each bout. Wiry little hamsters and impossibly fat hippos were waltzing about, trying to pull each other's limbs off. It was insane but delightful. Six Saturday nights at the wrestling reminded Julia how quite hopelessly silly, but harmless, people can be. Intellectual, no, but an insight into the funny, allowably absurd human condition.

There is nothing in the idea of being open to suggest you must fall in with the people or the things you open up to. That might even set you back in your development. If you have some unresolved hang-ups on specific issues, you may have to accommodate or suppress them until you wish to confront their power over you. The important step right now is to realize what is going on with you: 'I have hang-ups on this and that, but I want to understand why it is so.'

For example, you may have a 'moral' reason for not going to the races. Gambling! That side of life! Placing bets among seedy-looking people! Spectators getting excited over horses that lose more than they win, while others can't afford to go out at all! You might be internally correct in your judgements, but is that the final reality? Try going to the races, just once. Bet on a few nags. Take part in the proceedings as if you were playing truant from school. Study the form, and study the people. Witness what happens to them when they see their silly old horse lagging behind the rest. Watch them win. Watch the people studying the parade at the paddock. Eat a greasy hamburger with greasy onions. And watch yourself every moment. Experience all there is. When the day is done, ask yourself what you really feel about your previous views on racing and racing people. Be assured, God or your conscience will not zap you if you betray your allegiance to morality. He will be standing behind you in the queue, studying form, and watching to see which horse you think has class!

CHANGE YOURSELF FIRST — THEN THE WORLD

By giving yourself permission to depart from your usual judgemental routines and ways of thinking, you will begin to see your world a little differently. There will probably be no sweeping enlightenment, unfortunately, but there will be a realization that you are missing huge chunks of yourself by cutting off areas you decided were off-limits to your experience. Always strive to push out your perimeter fences; better still, find ways to break through them!

Tourists like to go on a two-week trip to some part of the world they see in a glossy, colour-coded brochure, for example. Guidebook and phrasebook in hand, they fly in, take a bus or taxi to the hotel, and they've arrived. Their itinerary takes them from hotel to beach to local shops, night-spots and markets, on the odd harried tourist excursion, then back to the airport. I remember asking friends how it went on one of those package tours, what they discovered about the country, the people:

'It was OK. The flights and buses were OK, a bit dirty though. Couldn't get a thing to eat. Always closed. The food was a bit strange; drinks were very expensive. Everything looked run down. I suppose there was a strike on or something. We just couldn't understand the people and their shops don't have air conditioning! Yes, it was a good trip. We'll do somewhere else next year maybe.'

I think all travellers fall into three classes: business, tourist and adventurer. Business people fail to notice where they are, due to their itinerary or preoccupation with representing the company. It could be the Raffles Hotel in Singapore, the Hilton in Bombay, or the Tropicana in Santa Barbara. Hotels and taxis have become identical worldwide. Tourists meanwhile are bored where they are now, and they have surplus money to throw at something. So a break away from the daily routine is as good as anything. Hence the sardine syndrome on popular resort beaches. Adventurers, on the other hand, set out on a quest, prepared for surprises. They might end up running a boatyard in Thailand, counting reindeer near Skoganvarre, or making the break from office mediocrity in Melbourne. Adventurers make no reservations; they just stay open and miss nothing.

Everyone is a potential adventurer, and you don't have to travel anywhere. Life is the journey, and you certainly have a ticket! Will you be satisfied with the package deal, the predictable, safe, unremarkable route? Or will you choose a challenging path that leads to fulfilment and success?

What if you were told that 80 per cent of you is unrealized, uncharted, missing? Send out the search party! Closed thinking restricts our view of the big picture, and our latent potential. Certainly, each person has their own realistic level of awareness and capacity to be open. But by opening more, we always increase our awareness and potential.

So begin your quest by being open. If you shut out possibilities from your mind, you end up with a small, limited mind. Open up beyond the obvious, and you will see there's much more for you than you have allowed. You will not be seeking your potential outside yourself. What you need is *already within you*. Grasping that will be your greatest step forward. Buying this book is a simple confirmation that you have an open mind. I have planned your journey carefully: we will examine your situation, your goals, and even the way you think. Each development milestone will increase your confidence, build your self-esteem, and open up exciting possibilities for you. You are already taking responsibility for your future. That's a very good sign!

REVIEW

1 You have grasped the idea of being in control of your life, and not subject to the will of others.

2 Instead of relying on the past, you can try new approaches without fear.

3 You have acknowledged all aspects of your situation – good and bad – now you can plan accordingly.

4 You realize that open thinking will generate fresh ideas to build your future.

3 Are You Aware of Yourself?

Attachments we once thought were vital to maintaining our being *are not*, we discover, and with that discovery it becomes not only possible but compelling to seek an honest unity within ourselves.

Gail Sheehy

OVERVIEW

We live busy lives, but often lose the essence of living through loss of focus. The reality of *being* can be disturbing to many people: it unsettles them.

Other people can 'define' us. This not only limits our scope, but may also cause us to 'disappear'. Deciding who we are can be surprisingly difficult. But we must be acknowledged as the people we truly are, and achieve what we want in life from that unique point.

The importance of feelings is stressed here, for it is through feelings (and not the intellect) that we can fully celebrate our life experience. The concept of the individual being at the centre of events gives a focus for later work.

THE PERILS OF STAYING BUSY

Whatever your lifestyle, you would probably admit that life in general can be very busy. Even if you are spending your days in prison, there is a daily routine to occupy your time. On television soaps we often watch busy executives jetting around making fantastic deals, then rushing home to their busy families. No matter how busy they all are, they

still find time for affairs, scandals and complex intrigues. In less glamorous settings – the real world – there are men and women caught up
in the daily grind of simply living and hopefully keeping their heads
above water. There are overloaded mothers coping with work, taking
children to and from school, shopping, entertaining friends, trying to
stay trim with Jane Fonda tapes blasting away. There are frantically
busy men aware that company takeovers, technology and younger col-
leagues might displace or unseat them. Busy, busy, busy, but hardly
focused.

How often do you get a real break from a busy mind? Trying to sleep
with a busy mind is one situation we are all familiar with. Problems,
bad recollections of the day's events, reminiscences over past relationships, all fluttering about like crazed birds the cat brought into the
house. Sometimes there's a silly tune you can't drop from your consciousness. You look at the clock. Three a.m. Maybe a visit to the
bathroom. You'll be drained tomorrow. These are symptoms of a busy
mind, refusing to settle.

Of course, the busier we are in general terms, the less time we have
to think about life and its undisclosed possibilities. Why spend time
contemplating your navel when there are films to see, people to visit,
cars to drive, boats to sail, paths to jog, money to earn and worries to
entertain? Being perpetually busy keeps our minds off things, and that
can't be bad. (Or so we hope.) Whenever the basic questions of 'Who
and what are you?' arise, you answer by saying something along the
lines of 'It's time I did the ironing or the oil change, it's overdue.' But
passing time is not creative living. Boredom and dissatisfaction actually
arise from avoiding effort, even if that effort would mean achievement.

THE ESSENTIAL YOU

The quiet moments cause the most trouble! If you are very unfortunate, you may experience short flashes of 'presence'. In other words,
you suddenly become aware of where you are and what you are experiencing. You may be standing on the bus, for example, thinking 'This is
me on the bus, and I feel conspicuous.' Have you experienced episodes of
self-consciousness where you seem to be observing yourself? When
suddenly you take notice of yourself taking notice?!

Accidents are good at bringing us into the immediacy of the
present. Crises in our lives put us outside ourselves, as if we were a
spectator at our own tragedies. Even if you cut a finger while peeling
onions, there is an awareness of your own body; blood leaks from it,

and your concern focuses on the moment. It vanishes of course, as you race to find the sticking plaster and human comfort. Fortunately there are other, less violent ways to discover we are really here.

Our presence on this Earth is quite often defined or substantiated by other people. The people around you have decided who you are and what makes you tick, at least to the limits of their interest in you. They have even specified rules of behaviour which you have grown into. How helpful people really are!

But are you aware of what the essential you is? Take your notebook again and describe yourself using clear headings, adding detail if you wish. Ask yourself if the statements are truly your own, or reflections from other people. Once you've done this, you'll see two groups of statements emerging: one that suggests role conflict, the other, the real you. To help you get the idea, use the following prompts in the same way as before:

You: Possible Role Conflict
I'm good-natured.
> People are always coming to me with their problems, but they never listen to mine.

I'm no good at making decisions.
> I never really get the chance: someone else usually takes over.

I am cynical about everything.
> People like my cynical sense of humour – it gets a laugh, but I have no wish to live the life of a misanthrope.

You: The Real Version
I like the feeling of being a good parent.
> I enjoy the idea of helping another grow physically and mentally.

I thrive on chaos.
> Certainty bores me.

I like change, new people and places.
> I like to think I'm a creative type because I avoid routine.

Can you see how many of the things you have listed are truly you, and how many are based on how other people perceive you? You are known for the things you have listed. And you perpetuate other people's opinions of you through the consistent practice of the things you do, and the values you transmit. You communicate signals that people pick up. And signals can be misleading. They often relate only to specific people, contexts and environments. For example, eating out, you may be perceived as a fusspot; at home, a slob. Your workmates see you as reliable, true to the company and a great person to be with; at home, you might be a broody, self-centred troublemaker that people in their right mind should avoid. Socially, you might be a friend to all in hotel bars, but the poisoned misfit that causes social clubs and neighbourhood committees to disband. When we try to understand how other people see us, we catch various glimpses of what they think we are really like. It is indeed a series of conflicting images in a wobbly mirror. Quite often, we believe in the wrong reflected image. That's when we need to look closer.

There is a real danger in allowing other people to define what we are and limiting us as a result. It can develop to extremes. For example, I remember an employer who was dumbfounded on hearing that a certain man was an accomplished public speaker in local politics. The poor fellow was kept out of sight in stores because they thought he was a mouse. His self-projection *at work* was mouse-like, so *a mouse he was!* Perhaps his first week at work went badly and the patterns were set: other people *gave him* a suitable personality.

RE-PRESENTING YOURSELF

It would be nice to tell people that we are not mice; and for them to give us a fair chance to be ourselves. The main problem, of course, is that often we have really not decided what we want to be known *as*. Our image and identity have been built since childhood, and for the most part, we have allowed it to happen, seeing no reason for change. Rather than question how our image was developing, it was easier and less troublesome to have others reflect possibilities that were near enough to make no difference. This is acceptable when we are young, but can become an identity crisis in later life. You are presently exploring the reality of change, and how the future is going to see you, are you not? So look ahead with the conviction that you are unique and worthy of attention as *yourself*, not as a faulty reflected image!

The pressures to satisfy another's image of you are tremendous, but doing something *as an individual* now and then brings you back to the reality of you actually *being* here. Why not perfect a hobby, join a self-help group, complete further education, sing in a choir...? (What have you got to lose?) Sudden complete changes in attitude or behaviour will naturally strain your relationships with others, and will certainly raise a few eyebrows, but it seldom happens this way, fortunately. Your self-growth will be more ordered and will allow for transition.

Remember, though, that other people like to see you just *so*. It makes life simpler for them. Once they have established and fixed who you are, they can deal with you over and over again, without having to start from scratch. It is a social convention, but it stifles vitality. People do it to us, and the worst thing of all, *we do it to ourselves*. Please appreciate the significance of this. Learn how to break into the loop somewhere so you can take control and act independently.

To see in more detail how this stereotyping works, let's look at an 'average' couple discussing their marriage with a counsellor:

Janet: My marriage has gone stale. I'm well aware that I married too young. I should have studied or something. I liked art. Perhaps I could have become a commercial artist with an advertising agency...

John: I thought she was terrific; that's why I married her. We had fun in those days, real fun. Then we had the kids, I took a job that paid almost double, we took the plunge with bigger houses and now look what we have. It all seemed right, what else would we have done?

Janet: I'll be 36 next month. I certainly don't *feel* old. But I don't think I like myself as I used to. My husband is a good provider; I doubt if he even considers other women. He sees me as someone who organizes the house; I'm a social necessity. All *he* needs to do is work away and give me money for the hairdresser's or winter boots.

John: The kids drain me now; they're challenging me all the time, and it interferes with the work I bring home. I'm bored with women who talk houses and dishwashers and soap powders. Recently I feel trapped, doing the same old things and being taken for granted. Nobody wants to hear about my frustrations at work. I'm getting no satisfaction or fun out of life. It just goes on.

Janet: Friends make it clear they don't want to hear my problems. They'd rather talk about soap powders or refrigerator capacities. There's *got* to be more than this. I must be good at something. I wish I could find the energy to concentrate on finding a way. Honestly, I'm tired.

John: She seems to have lost interest. I work away, trying to keep my end up at least. What more can I do? Somehow, the things we worked for seem less important to us now, but we couldn't quite do without them, could we?

Janet is convinced the marriage is at the centre of her problems. She laments her lost opportunities. She loosely blames her husband and her friends for being so shallow. She blames the system for stacking the odds against women. Though the time has come to do something, she has no commercially recognizable skills or earning capacity. She has no clear ideas on how to set or achieve concrete goals. Her age is on her side, though. She could learn the skills she needs to fulfil herself, and could choose to avoid women that make soap powders their level of fascination, and find new friends.

John is no better off. His providing role has gone too far along the same old dreary path. The goals the couple had set originally were relevant, but they have become inflexible and ingrained. John's life is work and more work. Affluence, comfort, and yet more of the same. His career has no doubt served the family well, but even he is coming to doubt the ongoing value of that. It looks good on paper and presents well to like-minded friends, but it's become rather boring.

What has actually happened here is less obvious than these surface problems, and will take much more effort to solve. The husband has reached an understanding of his wife over many years which basically suits him. He's the provider; he probably likes his work, frustrations aside. Other women aren't his scene. He has the basics in place (lovely wife, kids, house, job, good standard of living, lifestyle). He feels satisfied that his wife talks to other women about harmless things. Everything seemed safe, but he now feels less secure about the future and his role in it.

The wife has lost herself somewhere along the way. Her husband's identity is probably well established and visible at work, but her identity has been sacrificed – willingly, if unwittingly. Has she explained her feelings of stagnation as a person to her husband? Is he aware of the sacrifice she has made for their cosy but boring lifestyle? Is she aware of how he feels, willingly providing for all, but nevertheless feeling trapped? Both partners' needs and hopes as individuals have been frustrated, but like most things in life, individuals are responsible for making choices and taking action.

The sad thing about this 'average' couple is that both partners assumed they were doing the right things for so long. They created each other's roles and they acted them, as they were expected to. Following the script was the easy option. The status quo was being maintained, and so undoing all this, or questioning motives, would have caused pain. How often we avoid pain, only to suffer worse consequences! The Open Person realizes that nothing is perfect, but with a creative approach, manages to improve on imperfection. This requires a strong sense of self (which you will develop!)

RE-DISCOVERING YOURSELF

Can you shake off the imaginary you that's ingrained so deeply? Is there such a thing as a fresh start? Of course there is! The first step is to determine who you are inside, then promise yourself to be flexible about the next steps. Your age or circumstances are immaterial. A vital part of this exercise is establishing the awareness of presence: 'I really am here.' The situation of trying to be someone else, or squeezing yourself into some convenient mould, is unhealthy. We need to be acknowledged as the people we are, to enjoy being alive, and to achieve something with what we have. Whenever you are misrepresented, compromised or ignored, say so. Speak up and justify your precious space!

When you are about your everyday life, are you aware of the realities of the moment? Have you concrete feelings of being? Yes I know it's abstract, but think about it. For example: I am reading this book, I am talking, I am peeling potatoes, I am flying an aircraft, I am being an utter fool, I am kissing my lover, I am in a taxi with strangers, I am crying, I am laughing, I am feeling depressed...you might call it the 'this is it' reality. Good, bad, happy, sad – whatever is happening to you at the moment, now, any time. Experience it completely. Savour it like the smell of fresh baking.

Now, what have you learned about the essential you, compared to your earlier assessment? Imagine yourself attending an interview, but not for a job. Let's say it's some research on the way people present themselves. After an hour of discussing yourself (in any way you think appropriate), what would the panel's notes look like? Write up some quick notes from their side of the table. Did you see yourself sitting there? Did you hear the awkward things you decided to tell them? What sort of person were you: how aware, how straightforward, how well represented? What did you add up to in the panel's eyes? The question which stems from this may give you cause to wonder. Do you see yourself differently from how others see you? Remember how you defined yourself earlier. Try to pin yourself down and paint the picture.

LIVING IN THE MOMENT

If you rush about all day, forever occupied, distracted and 'involved', you will miss the whole point of being in touch with the moment. Too much rushing and you'll lose yourself in the whirlwind. How much of your time is really wasted, should you look at it objectively?

Or, if not exactly wasted, are there periods of time which give you very little in terms of being that specially unique person, you?

Making money and spending it might make you happy in a general 'instant gratification' sense, but is the process a deep and moving joy to you? Similarly, you might play tennis because people like you should play tennis. But what if you'd rather be gardening, playing the bag-pipes or reading the works of Tolstoy? Is this truly living your own life? Even when you are doing the right things, are you giving it your best and taking full satisfaction from it, celebrating its essence?

Think about your feelings whenever you do anything. You will find you even have feelings cutting grass with a lawn-mower, or watching a sparrow playing in a hedge. These things, trivial as they are, should not be dismissed as trivia unworthy of a place in your consciousness. You feel and you are alive because of it. It isn't possible to learn how to feel, in the same way we learn how to perform a job of work. But it is possible to acknowledge what is happening inside yourself, as a result of experiences around you.

Feelings only exist and develop in consciousness when we allow them to gain expression. Total censorship of our feelings might mean censorship of good and bad: we suppress undesirable feelings in the lows of our lives, but suffer the blandness of never revelling in the good times. Self-awareness and feelings – good and bad – are complementary. Isolate feelings from consciousness and you become more and more an un-person. So you can see that openness and self-awareness are avenues to a better, more conscious future. They expand your worlds – external and internal. Now that can't be so terrible, can it?

SELF – AND OTHERS

When in a crowd, do you feel lost in it? Do you feel self-conscious, detached from it in some way, or even feel superior to it? People in a crowd can feel lonelier or more conspicuous than on a mountain-top. If you were called on to make a fund-raising speech at a community gathering, would you feel their eyes on you? The awareness of self is often intensified by situations such as these. Don't fight it! You exist! Your self-consciousness is real, valid and natural.

There are also times when you can feel larger than life. Perhaps you believe strongly in a cause and canvass passionately for justice; or a hard slog produces an excellent piece of work and you experience deep fulfilment. In each case, you may be totally surprised by your energy, your quality of judgement, and your power of self-projection. You are amazed that it came out of you! A great feeling indeed.

'Self' as a concept is commendable. If you feel invisible sometimes, then you must reassert yourself. But be mindful of over-reacting, for others may find you arrogant and self-centred! We all operate in a world with other people. So if we behave like isolated and conceited prima donnas, the enriching process of interacting with others will be denied to us. It's like splashing around in a pond with four sides labelled 'consciousness', 'world view', 'environment' and 'conditioning'. We make our waves, and they radiate from us. Reflected waves from the sides are predictable, but sadly limited, and limiting. But by interacting with others in the pond, we experience rich patterns from their experience and corresponding reflections. We must be aware of ourselves, but we must remember to be aware of others also. Personal growth cannot occur in isolation: we need healthy interaction and productive stimulation.

YOUR LIFE, NOT THEIRS

Life can be seen as absurd nonsense, or a thrill. You may drift along if you want, but drift along properly. When things happen around you, take it all in. Don't limit your encounters only to good things: we can learn so much from troubles also, even if the experience runs us ragged. Examine your feelings and acknowledge they are there. If a film makes you sentimental, and you allow that feeling to flood your consciousness, let it enrich you. Don't question your motives or deny yourself the chance of learning through direct experience. Limit emotion and you limit experience, creativity, life. Through feelings, you give yourself clear evidence that you are here, rather than rushing around merely coping with life. Laugh at yourself, whatever your predicament. Study situations when they go wrong, and patiently monitor events for things you might normally miss. When you do that, you are opening up your creative, innovative side, and life is less difficult, less overwhelming, more generous.

Be assertive when you must be assertive; don't let people walk all over you. But never slip into aggression – that is unproductive and unhealthy. Explain things to those who need to be informed of how you feel, what you think. It is so much easier in the long run growing as we go. Major overhauls are stressful and usually costly in terms of fall-out. Don't deny your feelings or your presence in any situation, even while allowing others the same. Politely refuse to fit into the rigid patterns of others, just to keep the peace or make life easy. Why live your life if you cannot honestly say it is yours?

Being you is easy, and yet it's the most difficult thing! You can go on as you have been doing, or you can reach for the stars. You are at the centre of all you are, haven't you noticed? You will have setbacks and problems trying to get this right. But the effort in trying will be rewarded. Your desire to be fully in touch with yourself must come before hopes, goals and ambitions. Otherwise, you are off to a false start. But you are not empty-handed. The power to attain is within you. The time to begin is today, in preparation for tomorrow. So let's press on with your new-found awareness of self and matching enthusiasm!

REVIEW

1 You have detached yourself from the everyday demands and business of living; you appreciate the need to 'centre' yourself and value life.
2 Rather than others deciding who you are, you now make the decisions.
3 The first stages of self re-creation have become clear to you.
4 You have learned to trust feelings as being valid guides.

4 Preparing a Material Inventory

We make a living by what we get, but we make a life by what we give.

Winston Churchill

OVERVIEW

It is a useful exercise to take stock of our worldly possessions. We gather them, but seldom ask ourselves what they are worth and what they mean to us. By establishing our present situation we can then determine what we might want. Since goal-setting will include material goals, a clear starting point must be identified.

Our income and associated lifestyle form part of the audit. No 'contentment benchmarks' are offered, but there is a call for reflection on what material worth means to an individual. Some myths about money and possessions are examined.

MATERIAL WORTH

The idea of this chapter is to define your material worth in some detail. It will help you to assess your attitudes towards the possessions you have, and those you may want to have. There is no scoring system as such; you are simply taking a good look at the material aspect of your life. Include everything that has tangible value (but don't labour over the possible value of your vast butterfly collection). While playing the accountant, take time to reflect on what it all means to you. Do you think you want lots more material possessions, or would you happily give some away?

IN PURSUIT OF POSSESSIONS

We all gather things in our time here as we progress through our several phases: in childhood there are toys, games and novelties; in adolescence home computers, musical instruments and reading materials, possessions related to learning; then follow the electronic novelties, including hi-fis and cassette players. When we graduate to the more serious consumer years, the list is infinite. Advertising and social pressures feed the urge to consume, to participate in the pursuit of plenty. Hoarding possessions can become a weapon against personal insecurity – but, on the other hand, owning things can give us pleasure, comfort and a sense of well-being. Yet, as many people are becoming aware, materialism in itself does not necessarily improve the quality of life.

CONTENTMENT OR GUILT?

Regardless of the amount of information we have on the inequalities of our world, we must attend to our own affairs. In our everyday situations, we cannot be held responsible for civil wars, earthquakes, famines or disasters. But then we are welcome, as humans, to respond to such things in the world. Whether you are rich or poor is immaterial. If you want to help, please help. There is a surfeit of unfounded and unproductive guilt all around us. It is a human thing sometimes to feel uneasy about our relative prosperity and privileges, or our desire for them. This is something we all must cope with. If you are to make any sense of your material position, you must feel comfortable and grateful in the reality of owning things. Then consider what you are going to do about the world. Wallowing in the injustices of the world makes us miserable and does nothing to improve our individual or collective lot. So relax, and enjoy!

By the same token, if you have a humble but friendly little place of your own, or a very nice place indeed thank you in the best area of town, would you gladly share a small dilapidated cabin out in the wilds? Now there is nothing wrong with living in a small cabin miles from anywhere. If you are happy, it is ideal. However, if you are in a cabin, but would like a nice bungalow, don't feel guilty about it! That is the spirit in which we should embrace material things. Like them, but never exactly love them.

HARD NUMBERS

It is time to list your material possessions. Only you know what you have. What you must do is gather your thoughts and behave like an accountant. To give you some assistance in this exercise, refer to the Material Inventory balance sheet below. Follow the outlines given and tabulate or estimate the value of each and every thing you list. Should your items not fit the list as shown, improvise, but don't miss anything important. If you have a yacht moored off Monaco, don't forget to list that too. If it's a one-fifth share in a greyhound with premature atherosclerosis, put it down (but be kind to the dog). We are doing an audit of your net worth, whether you're in a mansion or a basement room.

Remember, net worth must consider the debts as well as the assets. (Now the truth comes out!) In the section on outstanding loans, list mortgages or other charges against your assets. There is no point hoping the loan from your brother will somehow go away, just because he earns more than you. *Don't live under illusions. Know the worst, face up to it, and plan accordingly.* (As an Open Person, you should have no difficulty being forthright.)

If you have been honest with yourself, you will have a very good idea of where you currently stand. Deduct your total liabilities from your assets (assuming all loans have been called in), and you now have your net worth for our purposes here. That is the first milestone in your Material Inventory. You have established some worthwhile facts about yourself.

MATERIAL INVENTORY: ASSETS

ASSETS   *AMOUNT OR ESTIMATED MARKET VALUE

Bank Account Deposits, etc.

Investments, Shareholdings
Family Residence
Second Home
Major Furniture and Furnishings
Boat, etc.
Vehicle(s)

Hi-fi Equipment
Television, Video Equipment

Appliances (refrigerator, washer, microwave)
Garden Equipment, Power Tools
Garage Equipment
Sports Equipment

Clothing
Linen, Bedding, Floor Coverings
Typewriter, Cameras, Binoculars
Personal Articles of Value
Musical Instruments
Jewellery
Luggage
Other

*Cash Value if Sold

(not original cost)

MATERIAL INVENTORY: LIABILITIES

LIABILITIES   CURRENT STATUS OF ALL LOANS, ETC.

Mortgage

Mortgage on Other Property
Car Loan
Loans on Consumer Goods
Credit Outstanding (Visa, etc.)
Credit Outstanding (Retail Stores, Mail Order)
Home Improvement Loan
Personal Loans (Family, Friends)

Outstanding Debts for Services Rendered
Borrowings for Investment or Business Purposes
Tax Liabilities Outstanding
Estate Settlements in Trust (Not Disbursed)
Gambling or Betting Debts
Liens on Property Through Bad Debts

Imminent Expenditures Committed or Known

(ASSETS LESS LIABILITIES = NET WORTH)

CASH FLOW

Just as assets less liabilities told you something, your monthly income less outgoings results in *net monthly excess*. Think about your monthly income from all sources: salary, state benefits, family allowance, bank interest, share dividends, moonlighting... Then consider where most of it goes: mortgage, rent, food, heating, car expenses, insurance, clothing, entertainment, pet food, loan payments, etc. The amount left after the deductions is your net monthly excess. (See balance sheet *Monthly Income and Expenses*, below.) Is it positive or negative? You probably have a budget tracking system in place already, so this exercise should be simple. Look up old payslips, bank statements and bills for the actual numbers – don't guess.

MONTHLY INCOME & EXPENSES

INCOME   RECEIPTS

Salary, Wages, Commissions from Sales

Part-time Earnings
Second Job
Partner's Employment
Income from Estate Settlement
Alimony, Maintenance or Other Court Payments
Pension
Income from Former Employers
State Benefits
Voluntary Payments from Relatives

Bank Interest
Investment Income (Share Dividends, Interest)
Rental Income (Property, Other)
Business Income

Other Receipts

_____

EXPENSES   MONTHLY OUTGOINGS

Mortgage, Rent
Car Expenses, including insurance
Food and Household
Heating, Lighting, Telephone

Maintenance of Property
Insurances
Entertainment and Social Expenses
Miscellaneous Outgoings

(INCOME LESS EXPENSES = NET MONTHLY EXCESS)

DON'T FORGET THE LESS OBVIOUS...

Are you employed? Would you call it a career or a job? Gainful work
is a substantial component in our self-perception and position in life.
If you are unemployed, you are still required to take part in this
assessment – unemployment is merely a state of not having a job or
doing gainful work. So, working or not, what does work mean to
you? Is it simply a case of regular money coming in, or does it repre-
sent status? Does it satisfy you completely, or are you generally at odds
with work? In general terms, what value do you place on work? Give
this more than a quick thought, and try to focus on the potential of
work as a real asset, not just its present value.

Also remember that tangible things are not simply possessions that
can be turned into hard cash. The potential to make money and translate effort into possessions or cash flow is a hidden asset most people
ignore. In two years' time you may be earning twice what you are
now! (For our purposes here though, don't list 'potential' assets or
tentative pay increases.) But cheer up. Even if your numbers on paper
look sad, remember that you are your own best asset!

THE BOTTOM LINE AND LIFESTYLE

What is your lifestyle? That is as diverse a question as there are people.
If your net worth and your net monthly excess are both looking very
sorry, don't despair! This exercise was planned to bring you to a true
and impartial understanding of your material situation. I have no hidden agenda to place you above or below some arbitrary benchmark.

Depending on how positive or negative your net monthly excess is,
your lifestyle may be closely governed and measured by the economics
of money in, money out. But if you live frugally on a low income,
you might be as well off as the big spenders on big salaries. The real
difference is only one of scale, and probably the degree of personal
anxiety. If you are a company director in the top 500 group of companies, you can still feel miserable after this exercise. Quite often, top

people are the very ones to take unreasonably big risks to hit the big time. Their visible numbers on paper may be significant, but so might be their worry with the debt-load to keep up appearances. Whatever you may earn, *living beyond your means is not true success*. Any plausible citizen can collect loans and credit leverage. There is no competitive allusion here. This is simply a process of self-discovery and personal assessment at the most basic level: things. The process of assessing your material worth also determines your realistic lifestyle, however, based on current assets and earning power. Notice that no comment is being made on what you *should* have, or what ratios *must* be in place between capital assets and your expenditures. We are only establishing a point on your map.

ASSESSING YOUR MONEY FEELINGS

How do you *feel* about your net worth, your net monthly excess? Are you content, feeling really smug at how well-off you are? Do you feel vulnerable, subject to the least ill wind that could destroy you financially and every other way? If you lost your present monthly income, how long would it take before things would have to change significantly? Are your reserves in terms of years, months or weeks? How independent of the system do you perceive yourself to be? Are you mortgaged so deeply that you could lose your home should you be made redundant? If you are struggling along in the middle of a crisis at the moment, are you holding your own or steadily going down every week? Are you so self-sufficient that you are quite bored with money altogether, and would gladly become a weaver in some remote, idyllic spot, just to escape the nonsense of it all? To help you gauge your feelings to all this, you must tell yourself the whole story on paper – words and/or doodles. Writing the situation down concentrates your feelings beautifully.

You alone know where you stand right now. Be honest. Be angry if you wish. Be singularly complacent if you believe that this whole exercise has been tedious and beneath you. You are free to be whatever is appropriate. Some of you might have discovered how emotional you have become as a result of calculating your position, and might be taking time to think about it. Remember, the numbers themselves are only relative. It's how you *feel* about them that really adds up. Furthermore, understand that *you can do something to change your position*, if you so decide. In setting goals later, you will re-visit your feelings from this exercise.

Ask yourself if all those possessions and sources of income are important to you, or do they only add up to responsibility, worry, and fear of loss. Buddha said, 'The less you have, the less you have to worry about.' You don't have to be a Buddhist to see the truth in that. There is so much clutter in our lives. Separating the things you really want from clutter is an exacting task. This book will not lead you to a lifestyle or possessions that are not meant for you. What would be the point of that?

Examine your net worth and net monthly excess relative to the lifestyle you lead, and to the lifestyle you might want to lead. Try not to equate lifestyle with mere luxury and excitement. (Some very rich and successful people have very mundane hobbies. Conversely, some very unremarkable people have a love of exquisite things, whether they can own them or not.) It is a fallacy that the bottom line is *always* money. So pick out the ingredients for a customized lifestyle using imagination, not a calculator. True, some of the lifestyle ingredients might cost money, but think about budgets later. Meanwhile, dream!

BUILDING A MATERIAL LIFESTYLE

Stirring up your imagination at this point will whet your appetite for further study! Adding up your present situation is a useful exercise. But looking at possible lifestyle choices is also timely. Designing a lifestyle is refreshing, and fun!

As you read on, keep thinking about choices you would like to make. Don't be at all inhibited. Map out a rough lifestyle picture that would suit you; modify and focus it as you go. Don't just say you want to be rich – how rich would you like to be? Rough out something like this:

I live by the sea in a gorgeous house, mortgage-free. My finances give a basic living; they are topped up by six months' teaching. I enjoy my hobby of custom bicycle-building and going on annual adventure holidays. I have an ancient car but it runs well. The house is full of older furniture but the hi-fi and TV are top of the line...

So what is your lifestyle statement? No need to be too specific at this stage: you will write goals later, when the time is right. Just get the feel of it and get your confidence tuned up.

COMPARISONS DON'T PROVIDE REALISTIC MODELS

In drawing a lifestyle picture, however, remember there is a spiteful trap awaiting us when our logic leads us to blindly assume that someone else's lifestyle is better than ours. 'Oh, but they've got more money than us, they're on the up and up.' We inflict unhappiness on ourselves when we superimpose inappropriate values which embarrass our finite resources or aptitudes. This brings about a constant internal battle between our desires and our frustration at not getting them. Concentrate on yourself before you compare notes with what everyone else has, or does. You may fancy that fellow's Ferrari, but why? Why? Just because it's an unmistakable symbol?

There is also a dangerous and unproductive force in that peculiar trait of humankind, namely equating money, behaviour or things with status. A man wears a visibly expensive tailored suit, a mohair overcoat and a silk scarf. He is seen stepping into a smart white Mercedes, illegally parked outside a smart up-market shop. Why must we confer on him more status than Mr Average? Not content with that, passers-by feel they have more status than the van driver trying to park his rusty old vehicle behind the Mercedes. But all the while, the van driver is feeling particularly superior that day, relative to traffic police. Why must perceived status or 'money mentality' influence the passage of events, as experienced by the 'tiers' of people in this example? It's ludicrous! But all too often, false material values constrain us. We segregate ourselves into tiers and limit our perception of the bigger picture. The Open Person knows that status is fragile, but human potential limitless.

Net worth is a phenomenon of our vanity in many cases. It is also specific to a point in time. Keep your mind open to the whole picture. Fortunes and lifestyles have been lost through faulty decisions or social change. This book is not about to make you rich using some secret formula or sham hocus-pocus, nor does it prescribe money as the cure-all for human misery and restlessness. It will lead you only where you want to go.

If you have thought carefully about the searching interrogatories here, you will have recognized which path you are probably on. Right now, you know what things you have, and what those things mean to you. It's useful to have a starting point on your map: you know where you're coming from and where you might like to go. Later, we can examine specifically what you would like to have, what your own mark of success is. Isn't that a happy prospect?

REVIEW

1 You have determined where you stand in terms of net worth and monthly disposable income.

2 Your appropriate lifestyle has been clarified.

3 The process of self-discovery has highlighted your *feelings* towards money and possessions.

4 You are now able to assess your likely needs and material ambitions in the future.

5 Preparing a Personal Inventory

A curious feature of the ideal self is that a person who attains it does not necessarily rest on his laurels enjoying the self-esteem, but may revise his goals upwards – like a high-jumper who moves the bar up a notch.

Michael Argyle

OVERVIEW

Real success cannot be based on material things alone. Personal qualities and attitudes are vital to our overall sense of well-being. Knowing and understanding ourselves enables us to function properly with others. Rigid thinking may limit the full expression of our personal worth – hence the need to be open.

What are our strengths, our weaknesses, our problem areas? Leading questions which explore our personal attributes, maturity and direction will be asked. A list of desirable qualities completes this stage. The most significant breakthrough will be the realization that we can do *something* about our personal shortcomings.

WHAT SORT OF PERSON ARE YOU?

Believe me, the type of person you are is more important than your income or net worth. It is nice to have money and possessions, but if you are poor in personal attributes and qualities, real success will elude you. Even John D. Rockefeller discovered that. It is unlikely that you exist merely to gather more and more possessions, money in the bank, and endless equities around the world. Conversely, there is no call for any negative stigma about material things. In fact, by consuming, you are helping money to move in the economy and hopefully create jobs, directly or indirectly. But, that's right: there has to be more! Personal 'things' are just as vital to our sense of well-being and overall prosperity as things we can acquire or buy. In fact, they are a prerequisite to real success.

So, what sort of a person are you? Do people like you, or are you just fooling yourself about your popularity? Are you the person you want to be? It is possible you have areas of difficulty in coping with both other people and yourself. Is your ego in control of your behaviour, to your detriment? Are you at peace with the world? Do you suffer from stress?

The rain was really coming down as Jason approached the bank. Water droplets made his spectacles useless, and he tilted his head around to focus on the door handle. Inside, it was hot. His glasses steamed up at once. He could feel the sweat mingling with the droplets of rain on his face, and felt uncomfortable all over.

After 20 minutes of studying the various communication problems of everyone before him, it was his turn. He stood before the heavy plate security glass and said his piece in a discrete, subdued voice. His business was not for the whole world to hear. The girl mouthed something like 'Sorry, I can't...' so he tried again, louder, and closer to the glass. It made no difference; his voice was too soft to penetrate the glass. It was useless. He passed the books and papers through the sliding trough in the counter, but the girl still couldn't understand what he really wanted; it wasn't a cash withdrawal or anything simple.

Jason's mind raced ahead. 'Why must they isolate us by glass this thick? Why isn't there a speaking hole or something? A microphone? This is ridiculous! It's like an oven in here! Look at those people standing in line, like Polish housewives out for their bread and sausages! This is insane!'

Suddenly he realized the trough formed *a hole in the counter!* He placed his head down to it and began speaking into it. Immediately the girl sprang from her chair and withdrew to the back of the office. The lady at the next window also jumped. Robbery in progress! Code 211. Man threatening defenceless women across bank counter!

Sighing, Jason stood back and glanced at the queue, all the way out to the door now, with two neat zig-zags. They were all frozen with terror, their eyes fixed on his. Taking the floor like a demented orator, he spoke his lines to the assembled audience, loud enough to penetrate the thickest plate glass.

'Have I become Jaws, a giant mouse perhaps, maybe a vicious flea? What? This is the toyshop next door? Or the optician's? Oh, I see! The wrong shop! Don't mind me, I've just come to get my brain tested!'

He continued his performance with a complete description of the transactions he wanted to accomplish.

'I've just sold my house. I made 20,000 on that. My daughter's getting married so I need a transfer to my cheque account. I need a bank draft for 1200 to settle my debt with cousin Basil in Brazil. So there you have it. Everyone hear all right? Any questions?'

The atmosphere was intense; time had stopped. The assembly was transfixed, as if in collective prayer. Jason knew that he had lost control, but for the first time in his life he felt *powerful*. Even if he was to be escorted away to a little padded van, he knew this was his precious moment of abandon, his escape from conformity, the feeling of *being alive*.

If only we could behave like that – really open up our frustrated feelings, have a good laugh, then get our business done! In a sense, the unfettered part of our mind would prefer us to operate in a more open fashion, but we do have a certain social courtesy to maintain in the world. We are expected to behave ourselves in set ways, in each particular environment, and it would be fair to say we are different people in our everyday life situations, as discussed earlier. Crossing the very rigid boundaries from a socially unprincipled environment to a formal one, carrying badly chosen behaviour over, is usually disastrous. People always mistake inappropriate drama for sarcasm, cynicism, or plain aggression. It is essential to realize that we do have control over ourselves; the trick is to acquire the skill of proving it. Be open, but don't frighten people!

GETTING TO KNOW YOURSELF

You may not please all the people, all the time. That is an ongoing risk. But if we can find ways of relating to *ourselves* in a balanced way, then we are less likely to give little performances at the local bank. It might seem like a jungle out there sometimes, but be sure you are not growing rain-forests and their associated storms inside your own head. The dividing line between reason and the ridiculous is often blurred. At times we may miss some excitement or exceptionally good exchanges of humour because we are acting in too stiff and restrained a manner. That is a great pity, but take care where you draw the line between tact and letting go.

Underlying problems, created by bad experiences in the past, often cause us to have strong attitudes which result in excessive or irrational outbursts. Think of something that has upset you deeply. Document it on paper. Write out the facts in short story form. Bring out all the nasty things that happened, what people said at the time, and how you felt. Recall your reactions. Were they similar to our friend's in the bank, all drama but little real substance or hostility? Until you re-visit and quantify your bad experiences, you will be carrying a heavy load of luggage around with you. *Knowing and understanding* how you react, and why, is the essential first step in helping yourself.

WHAT IS YOUR VIEW OF THE WORLD?

Everyone has their own personal world view. This is your position based on your background, everyday situation, politics, spiritual feelings, ideas of happiness, exposure to information, and how people treat you. All of us, whatever shortcomings we believe we have in education and experience, have a general philosophy and basic understanding of even the most complex issues. Yet although the same things affect everyone, your specific perception may not be the same as the person next to you. Nobody has the 'right' perception, because we are individually experiencing life under different circumstances. And since our individual world views are so different, the combinations of perception and world view, together with our reactions to them, are staggering! Aberrations of perception cause separation between people, and hence what we believe to be right about some issue may be quite wrong, or at least distorted. Consider these approaches to 'other people':

Other People
> Know more than I do.
> Are more attractive.
> Are more successful.
> Have better contacts.
> Have more fun in life.

Other People
> Are basically stupid.
> Are losers.
> Are out of touch.
> Aren't as smart as me.
> Are of no interest.

It is quite easy to detect the errors of perception in both cases! Each view is flawed by polarization, by too wild an interpretation. Our own view of the world and attitudes to others might be just as hopelessly in error. If that is so, we must first come to realize this and then consciously begin to balance our position.

Attitudes give shape to our world view, and our world view gives shape to our attitudes. Be aware of that in every situation you find yourself in. If you are a decided pessimist, an attitude based on losing your job twice through redundancies, or losing your matrimonial home to a scheming ex-partner, you may treat a constructive merger offer towards your business with suspicion and underlying contempt. Similarly, you may view any hope of arms reductions between the superpowers as futile and simplistic. Simple attitudes drive complex attitudes. Polarized judgements cause separation between people, and we get caught in the games of escalation. That solidifies attitudes and world views, making us excessively narrow-minded (and possibly miserable). Believe that the world is a nasty, selfish, unjust place, and it really will be.

BELIEFS AND WIN/WIN STORIES

Someone who believes that all people are fundamentally 'good', regardless of where they come from, on the other hand, will generally have sensitive and caring attitudes. Such people find a common bond with others, whether they are dear old folks getting off a bus or young vandals spraying a wall with aerosol cans. Without being simplistic, if we see the world as full of promise rather than problems, our attitudes will actually *heal* the negative aspects we encounter.

All this notwithstanding, we seem to like living our lives around our relatively fixed attitudes and world view. These structural mechanisms allow us to handle the daily process of hearing and seeing information, and dealing with others. Generally, we are surprisingly tolerant. We probably don't get too disturbed if our best friend takes the opposite view from us on an issue – we assume that their world view is wrong! It is less easy to be tolerant, however, when the opposing views of *groups* are considered. But even there, the effort must be made to understand the other viewpoint. Negotiation (not compromise) avoids these win/lose conflict situations, turning them into win/win success stories.

DON'T ARGUE WITH ME, I KNOW THE TRUTH

The endless search for truth and absolute values in our lives is a commendable goal, but despite what you may believe, it relies on debate rather than on fixed laws. Science has enjoyed increasing credibility in our recent historical timeframe; we accept (without much protest) that it is best at claiming and proving truth. But even astounding timeworn theories get thrown out every now and then in favour of better ones. Newtonian science has been challenged by relativity; who will supersede Einstein? The Big Bang theories on creation may have to be restated after the Hubble space-telescope data has been sifted.

In the field of psychology, to take another example, Freud was upstaged by Jung, and now the Gestalt school of spatial psychology (Maslow *et al*) has carried the science even further, as we understand the workings of the brain with more confidence. It's all good stuff, but no more than a sophisticated collection of moving targets. Yes, the concepts and findings do help us understand more. But we are dealing with a *continuum* rather than a single vault containing all the answers.

Therefore, *stop searching for a list of absolutes or a theory to fit your life into.* Just accept that there are many ways to describe the same thing, and don't miss the fun because you have *opinions* on everything. The notion of being 'right' is itself a moving target. Live through opinions and you will be considered arrogant, inflexible and self-restraining. (The bumble-bee isn't supposed to fly, but it does.) As you progress in your self-development, you will consciously cast off many of your opinions and alignments. They will seem heavy, limiting and superfluous to you. Truth will be *relative to you* and what you are doing, not something imposed by superior knowledge. Don't forget that little microchip implanted in you called free will! It's there for a purpose: to help you.

COMING TO TERMS WITH REALITY

Our ideas on *reality* are also tied in with attitudes and world view. Often it is difficult to know what we really do think. Ask someone in the street how their world view translates to their reality!

Usually, we establish contact with reality by noticing and experiencing things in our everyday affairs. We do not intentionally set out each morning determined to discover what it is that gives us purpose or makes us add up to a whole person. The process is not that simple. Reality is more than answers to questions like 'What can I expect this year?' or 'Why are they treating me like this?' It might be reasonable to assume that we cannot find the answers anyway, because we haven't framed the *right* questions. Timing is another factor: we might not be ready.

In order to make any sensible comment on life we have to really *experience* it. Very often, we just have to patiently sit there at the cross-roads (location, situation, relationship or job), letting time go by.

Remember to be open to experience. Your attitudes, feelings and world view will determine if the experience is worthwhile or not – and the final judgement is relative to you alone.

The road outside is unusually busy today. People late for meetings are trying to get through. It's windy again; low clouds give the impression the world is moving through space. A strange feeling. Like two trains in a station. Which train is moving?

A rusty chimney pipe is stayed by four rusty guywires. I can see a heat-haze from it. Two women in the office across the road are exchanging snapshots, laughing; they light up cigarettes. In the next office, their supervisor is looking at the business paper.

Two lanes are blocked now, in both directions. The world has slowed down again. It is Tuesday. Another Tuesday. Another year killed in this dreary office. It really isn't good enough; reality has become a rut. Something has to change...

Once we discover our own reality, that doesn't mean we're cornered: *we can change our reality*, by following the conscious future path. You will develop a strong, intuitive sense of *knowing* when to make changes, and how to turn situations around. And the more skilled you become, the less time will be wasted in isolating causes and implementing remedies, for you'll get it right first time.

WE ARE SELDOM PERFECT...

Is a personal inventory vital to your progress? Well, without it, you may be unaware of flaws in your personality and behaviour that limit your potential. We tend to suppress our personal shortcomings because we know there's a lot of pain involved when we disturb the murky waters deep inside us. Unfortunately, this means we rarely know how to identify and measure the qualities we have, or do not have. You can count money on a table and write down the total. But can you count your *personal worth* and embellish it with facts in the same way?

It is extremely difficult to be open about our personal strengths and weaknesses. We fluctuate between flushes of greatness (the good qualities) and torment (the real nasties). Be honest with yourself. Your personal inventory is a mixture of some good personal traits, some you know could be better, and a set that you may attribute to a hostile demon lodged deep inside you!

There is often confusion over what we must do to perfect good qualities. Perhaps you would like to be known as considerate and agreeable. So you set out to be considerate and agreeable with family, friends and work associates. However, driving to work, you 'fight for your rights' in traffic, and when other drivers make mistakes you 'punish them' by harsh language or actual harassment. *Where* must the good qualities be exercised, developed and tested? Answer: *everywhere*, all the time, every situation! Be conscious of that and learn all you can *all the time!*

You are well aware that material success alone is shallow and unsatisfying without personal qualities you can be proud of. You want to *feel* good when you count your money and sail your yacht! People that come into your life want to feel that you are a decent person, unlikely to plot against them, or let them down because you are forgetful, indecisive and unreliable. And you want consistency, not a split personality, so your qualities must be universally applied wherever you go. What you are aiming for is a material-personal lifestyle combination that will *expand your reality* and, as you circulate, *expand the possibilities of your world.*

GET SOMETHING DOWN ON PAPER

Once we commit thoughts and facts to paper, we start to establish contact with ourselves. You did it for your financial Material Inventory. Counting money was relatively easy, wasn't it? Now try the same exercise with your personal qualities. Use a pencil and have an eraser standing by. You will make lots of mistakes! But don't erase the truth about yourself. You are not going to share your worksheets with anyone. So that gives you freedom to open up. Before proceeding with the interrogation, write a short autobiography of about 400 words. Start with your childhood and work forward. Pace it out so that your last 10 years get about 60 per cent of the words. Your story should include facets of your education, family life, major relationships, outline of work history (but not a detailed career report), interests, and the type of person you think you are. Finish with a statement about your immediate situation, dilemma, crossroads, or whatever.

Now review what you have written, and ask yourself if you are on the mark, or if your assessment looks like sugary self-inflation. Are you really in that autobiography? Take the time now to revise it and cut out useless facts about how well you handled that interview five years ago, or the nonsense about archery changing your world view. We often read the biographies of the famous. Ah, but it's nice to read even a modest essay on the most famous person in the entire world...YOU!

Next, consider the following questionnaire. It will help you draw a reasonably comprehensive sketch of yourself. There is no need to write out the list – just concentrate on the answers. There is no time limit, so consider each question without an eye on the clock. Take an interest in this; you are trying to communicate with yourself. If you don't think it's worth the time or effort, then you are essentially denying yourself a chance to grow.

PERSONAL REVIEW

Scoring System

Absolutely	(4)
Usually	(3)
Occasionally	(2)
Not the case	(0)

1 Personal Attributes

Can you tackle most problems with a fresh outlook and come up with smart ideas?

Are you self-confident in the sense of being able to handle any situation without going to pieces?

Are you persistent in getting things done, even if it's an uphill struggle?

Do you assume responsibilities easily and happily?

Are you courteous to people at all times, in all situations?

Are you independent (i.e. good at functioning alone)?

Do you make decisions easily?

Are you a good communicator?
  Written?
  Oral?

In your dealings with people do you allow for the range of human differences?

Are you willing to accept the other viewpoint?

Have you intuition and sensitivity to things that are not said or communicated by normal means?

Do you consider yourself good at your job (even if you are not entirely satisfied with it)?

Can you be assertive without over-reacting?

Do you adapt quickly to change and move on from there?

2 Interpersonal Maturity

Do you gain trust and respect from people with relative ease?

Are you willing to listen for extended periods without giving your point of view?

Can you win people's confidence and then willingly form a team around you to solve a problem?

Do you find it easy meeting new people?

In a work environment?

Socially?

When an argument develops into a row, do you slow things down and continue to its conclusion, rather than find a way of escaping?

Can you moderate your own anger?

Are you secure in your relationships?

Partner?

Peers?

Family members?

Do you honestly forgive people who rub you up the wrong way?

Are you patient?

Do you avoid getting worked up by news items or controversial topics of conversation?

Are you anxious about having a good try in all situations?

3 Direction

Is your life full of purpose and fulfilling at present?

Do you accept that certain things about you could be changed for the better, if you really wanted?

Do you believe that you are in control of your life, rather than being subject to every negative development from the external environment?

Is the idea of being ambitious compatible with your desire for security?

Do you agree that your experiences and achievements in the future need be only slightly affected by your background?

Do you make decisions routinely and easily, free of anguish?

Do you think that making a plan for the future is worthwhile, (even if you know what you basically want)?

SCORING POINTS

ASSESSMENT

135–144   Really? Go back and make sure you are being open with yourself! Otherwise, congratulations!

100–134   High achievement potential. Sound personal qualities and a sense of direction give you the required flexibility, tenacity and style to handle constructive change. You think positively and independently.

75–99   Some blind spots and interpersonal skill deficits; otherwise reasonably balanced. Perhaps you have strong opinions on issues which make you less flexible than you could be. You are relatively ambitious, but aware that you need to push yourself.

60–74   Time to get to know yourself better and plan some changes. A low score does not mean that there's little point in applying yourself. Improvement is certainly worthwhile, wherever you start from. Put yourself to the task. You will surprise yourself!

Below 60   Sounds like you're being hard on yourself, or you need to take stock. Your self-image seems to be needing some maintenance (we'll get to that later in the chapter). Perhaps you have placed yourself in confrontation with life, rather than in harmony with it. Your personal development may have suffered from a setback, or from poor support. But now is the time to do something. Now. This book will show you how.

4 List the skills you have, without restricting yourself to past or present work experience. Dealing effectively with people is a skill; so is building ornamental rabbit hutches.

5 List any special skills, or unique talents: amateur tree-doctor, closet poetry writing, retouching old photographs, special rapport with young children or restless youth...

6 What things in life give you the most *lasting and satisfying* returns? This is wide open. Bringing up children, splitting atoms in a linear accelerator, pigeon fancying, climbing the career ladder by sheer effort, spending money on creative hobbies, travelling to unlikely places, discovering your higher purposes, building a special relationship...?

7 Which direction do you feel you are going in at present? Is it a path of total stagnation and despair; a haven of stability and sufficiency; or one that offers some growth, maybe some real changes for the better?

8 How cynical a person are you regarding the process of learning and applying feedback on yourself? Are you above all that?

In this exercise there is no list of right answers that suits everyone! The score you added up is a helpful indicator though. What's your verdict on yourself? Did you have any interesting thoughts and feelings during your probing? It would be nice to have a snappy little checklist to see how unbalanced or unsatisfactory we are! However, only you can set standards: you will know where you would like to be. Record these ideas for future reference.

It takes effort to build up a comprehensive picture of yourself, and the medium of this book can only prompt you to open up to yourself. If you are wanting to progress, be willing to put in some work. Consider the skills you listed. Did you learn them at a single sitting? I think not. They demanded time and effort just as this exercise does. The Personal Review exercise gives you the chance, in the privacy of your own space, to construct a reasonable, open and honest image of yourself. These notes are your notes. If they are honest and to the point, you are serious about yourself. If not, give yourself a second chance and apply yourself more diligently. It will pay off in the end.

FIND YOURSELF BETWEEN THE LINES

The wonderful thing about humans is that they have certain acquired faculties built in that help to quantify things. Our eyes and our brain work together to warn us that a car cannot be driven through a space that is simply too narrow, for example. Similarly, we know very quickly if we have offended someone or lost their trust. We can read letters from partners, lovers, children, parents, business associates and friends, and the words don't say it all, but we *read between the lines*.

You have just finished answering some questions, and presumably you have made the effort to do your best and be honest. Re-read your notes. *Read between the lines*. Add facts and feelings you missed. Give your exercise life, and understand what it is saying to you. Then summarize your thoughts on the matter.

WHAT QUALITIES ARE YOU AIMING FOR?

To help you imagine what an all-round balanced person might look like, some attributes and qualities are listed here. The list can never be complete, because each of us perceives 'good' qualities to be relative to 'bad' ones, and relative to our individual preferences. For example, honesty is often a relative thing. We all manipulate this loophole to suit everyday requirements, some more than others of course. (Does your boss realize all this self-improvement business is preparing you for your next job?) The practice of elasticity in terms of honesty does not imply that absolute truth is a myth. But our society places demands on us regarding truth. For instance, withholding information is seen as par for the course, if releasing it might harm others. Too much of this may cause actual lying, however. Examine the personal attributes and qualities with prudence. There may be other shades of grey. You will know what I mean.

COMMONLY RECOGNIZED PERSONAL ATTRIBUTES AND QUALITIES

Honesty	There is even honesty among thieves!
Patience	Everyone isn't running at your speed.
Focus	Lose focus, and your mind is everywhere.
Self-Respect	Why should I put myself down?
Attitude	You can get there from here.
Resourcefulness	Who said everything was provided?
Perseverance	It's easy to give up; who believes your reasons?
Curiosity	You never know enough. Stay interested.
Innovation	Why wait for others to come up with ideas?
Sincerity	People are helpful to open, faithful folk.
Sensitivity	There is more to people than molecules.
Feeling	Bottling emotion denies a key dimension.
Decisiveness	Procrastination achieves mediocrity.
Wisdom	Knowledge is interesting but this is better.
Vision	Dreamers are the ones to watch.
Order	A tidy mind can find what's required.
Disposition	Are you playing Hamlet or Falstaff?
Effectiveness	Results come to those who understand how.

After perusing the list of personal qualities, you might now have a picture of where you are, and where you might like to be. There are no prizes or reprimands for your situation. The key is to recognize the progress you have made in self-comprehension. Compliment yourself; you are doing nicely.

BUILDING A PERSONAL LIFESTYLE

Now consider how your integrated lifestyle would look in terms of career, personal qualities, leisure and so on. What elements would you find in that lifestyle, and why would they be important to you? Go on, think out a personal lifestyle!

SUPPRESSED BRUISES OF THE SELF-IMAGE

The self-image you have constructed over the years may not be entirely to your satisfaction. Over your lifetime to date, you have assembled many experiences, together with your perception of them. Along the way, people may have told you how pathetic you were, or what a complete mess you made of something. Some parents, siblings and teachers are positively skilled in it!

You may have built or drawn something as a child, only to experience laughter, which you took to be disapproval. Perhaps you completed a particularly difficult project at school or work, something you felt was a breakthrough and a joy to behold. Some authority figure then proceeded to criticize your project, until there seemed to be no useful purpose in even explaining the good points. Negative childhood experiences are particularly damaging and often produce severe (but well-masked) transference problems for the adult self-image. We are all affected somewhat by this, all candidates for some interesting analysis!

These harmful experiences are real. They happen, and they hurt our pride at any stage of our lives. We are usually in a position of weakness at the time, which makes the painful business more penetrating. 'That's the last time I help that demanding clown,' you say. Then you move on to more bad experiences and the pattern is set to continue: 'I don't help anyone now; they don't deserve it.' Some of us are more sensitive to those affairs than others. Very often, the sensitive ones are the most creative in the first place, and their individual achievement is thwarted by the stupid comments of fools. It is a tragedy of human nature, and to some extent we do it to each other all the time, often unconsciously.

The real tragedy of this lies in the strong residual damage to the self-image. Those with thick skins move on to the next project, oblivious to the damage inflicted by the last one. But how many of us have those thick skins? Very few, when it comes right down to it. Many hours of psychotherapy are spent finding the causes of neuroses, and far too many neuroses stem from long-forgotten damage to the self-image system. Even if the damage falls short of causing neuroses, it still carries great power. Lack of confidence and low perseverance are the results of self-image problems. Something has harmed (damaged) the individual: a teacher's ridicule (undermining confidence before peers); a manager's bitter criticism (destroying perseverance to finish a project). Perhaps you can recall something that fits the description of self-image damage. There is no need to be under its power forever; you can work through it and break its grip.

REBUILDING THE SELF-IMAGE

When past experience or distorted ideas about ourselves harm our present and our future, we must consciously rebuild our self-image as quickly as possible. Self-image governs your attitudes to everything you experience or do. When a person believes they are worthless, clumsy, shy, introverted and generally short of the mark, performance in everything obeys the negative image. Shy people, for example, stare at the floor and wring their hands; as they speak, their breathing is short, shallow and confused with the actual words coming out. Since self-image governs the proceedings, all the added extras like blushing, sweating, eye evasion and foot games reinforce the overall picture. 'See, I'm shy. You can tell, can't you? Just look at my contorted facial muscles and feel my clammy hands!'

I recall a seminar on interpersonal skills. The delegates were all different: extroverts, introverts, socialites and social hermits. By way of introduction, they were asked to discuss memories of their schooldays. Without exception, each person admitted to shyness, a feeling of persecution, and the fear of 'not belonging'. Imagine the surprise of the delegates, now in their professional adult years, each believing they were the odd ones all that time! We all suffer from shyness and not belonging, the difference lies in our approach to the problem and our subsequent behaviour. Even the most confident and sociable individual has experienced those feelings (sometimes overt confidence is a smokescreen to offset basic insecurity!) Don't assume that shyness (or any other problem) is yours alone, a handicap you must endure, while others are confident, fully-functioning, balanced and successful. You can be whatever you decide to be. It sounds incredible, but it's true.

Decide what is important for you, and be certain that yesterday has indeed gone. You are not a failure! Who told you that? Well, they were wrong! You are learning to understand your attributes, your shortages, and what may be lurking in the shadows. You can do *something* about those personal shortages, other than worrying over them and bending your life to fit a pattern which is less than you deserve. Look again at your Personal Review and the list of qualities you think are desirable. Which qualities do you desire most, and why? It's all there for you to think about. I am certain you *understand* yourself a lot better now. I think you'll possibly *feel* better too!

REVIEW

1 You have come to appreciate that personal qualities are more important in your 'big picture' than material things.
2 Understanding your attitudes and approaches to life has helped you remove blocks to your progress.
3 The reality of changing your situation has become clear to you; the choice is always yours.
4 You have reconstructed your self-image with qualities appropriate to your emerging personality.

PART 2
Where Do You Want to Be, in Spite of Everything?

FORWARD PASSAGE...
FROM NEGATIVE...

TO POSITIVE

'Oh, I know what I want. That's easy. But getting it, ah well...'

'I wish I was someone interesting; I'm pretty dull really.'

'Honestly, I don't know what I want out of life, not when I think deeply about it.'

'I've always found that life gives you what's coming to you. What I'd like doesn't come into it at all.'

'The way the world's going, you're lucky to survive at all. Asking more than that is ridiculous.'

'If I know what I want, then achieving it is merely the next stage.'

'I am absolutely unique and capable of self-creation.'

'It's simple: I can select what's required through careful reflection.'

'Fate implies we are all helpless puppets; I see myself holding the strings.'

'The world is really what you make of it; nothing more, nothing less.'

6 What Do You Want?

My life has been full of terrible misfortunes, most of which never happened.

Montaigne

OVERVIEW

Defining precisely what we want may be more difficult than achieving it! 'Creative wanting' requires a focused mind and clear decision-making. It is a highly personal affair: we all have preferences and tastes. Popular notions on what we should want confuse the process, so we need to be vigilant. There is little point in pursuing the wrong things in life, wasting precious energy that could be used elsewhere to advantage.

Self-confidence is an essential element in making right choices. An orderly and supportive approach to decision-making is followed here, using written exercises to uncover true desires, and the subtle difference between 'wants' and 'goals' is also explained.

FROM HERE TO THERE

You have now roughly established what material things and personal attributes you have. It is unlikely you are totally satisfied, whatever inventories you have presented. Already the panic might be rising in you when you reflect on how little you seem to have, or the personal qualities you have uncovered. But with this as a basis, you can go on to establish what you want. Asking someone what they want appears to be one of the simplest questions, whether it is directed to an adult or a child. But the problem lies with specifics, and that is far from simple.

In fact, defining what you want may be the hardest thing of all. It might even be harder than actually setting out to *get* what you want! How do we know our own mind and what it really wants for us (if that is actually where 'wanting' originates)? Is it the mind we must look to when preparing our list of wants? Can we rely on idle thoughts to tell us where we are going and what we need with us?

Honesty comes into play here, and this is inseparable from a developed sense of openness. It is vital that you end up with the right things, otherwise you will be chasing clouds in a thunderstorm. You alone can define what things you want in your life, and the external world will be virtually useless to you in that search. So don't start looking for your inspiration or guidance from popular trends or well-researched features in glossy magazines. Enjoy your involvement with the external world, for that is where you operate right now, but don't let your environment or your circumstances *dictate* what comes first in your life. If you are an Open Person, you will *know* why you want certain things.

I WANT, I WANT, I WANT

Children are impossible when it comes to what they want, and a great deal can be learned from how their realities function. Take two children to a large department store on the Saturday before Christmas! Their minds will be busy, to say the least, and what you will see will be a study of human behaviour – in miniature, but superbly focused. Children's limited attention span prohibits them from making constructive proposals on what they *really* want. So in the department store, each moment leads to a new moment, and the kids buzz around from toy to toy, from games to pink rabbits to computers. Their little thoughts are directed at the fulfilment of big desires. Money doesn't come into this scenario! And if we explain limitations – lack of money, items too big or too old for them, poor quality – the children will get impatient and hostile.

Of course, as we get older, we supposedly get wiser. We hopefully begin to realize that things we accumulate, like toys in our childhood, do not bring with them lasting joy and contentment. It is a fact of life that material things will one day leave our lives altogether, even if it is only when we die. But as I said before, we can like possessions without falling in love with them. Wanting *indiscriminately* is pointless, but wanting *creatively* should bring us a healthy measure of well-being.

WANTING IN THE MIND

Don't be fooled by your mind, however well-intentioned it appears. Your mind is preoccupied trying to sort your affairs out. It can send little messages to you: 'Look, I'm doing my best to get you all I think you want, but things are tough in here. Besides, you don't help me too much. So I'll teach you a lesson. I'll make you miserable because you're not getting all I think you should have. So miserable you'll be convinced you're a failure. Serves you right. I'm whacked doing all your thinking and wanting for you, and even more whacked worrying for you about things not working out!'

You may not have heard your mind complaining, but do you recognize the feeling? Then again, perhaps your lively, constructive mind comes up with a generous thought like 'I think it's time you were made a partner in the company.' Somehow the partnership doesn't materialize. How will your mind react to the bad news? 'You're a failure! There's a conspiracy going on, let's track it down! Life is unfair, unjust, show them your anger.' Your mind works overtime to substantiate and justify every angle, to cast up every frustrated dream. This all seems abstract, but listening to the chatter of your mind can lead you a merry chase. Thoughts, feelings and desires can all go off like fireworks thrown on a bonfire, without warning, reason or order.

To go back to wanting, simply wanting for wanting's sake is hollow. Consider the children. You might buy them every single thing their little minds told them they 'wanted'. But they would be studying (and wanting) even more things, while the first load of items was being wrapped! Ask for their updated list of wants one week later. It will be as long as ever. I want to guide you away from novelty and the relentless search for gratification. I want to make you more discerning. I want to see you succeed with choices that are perfect for you!

Our unfocused minds alone are unreliable guides in the formulation of realistic 'want plans'. That is why we are not rushing into jotting down your goals now, so you can be quickly on your way to creating your own personal want list. Your mind sometimes says you are hungry after you've polished off a fine dinner and the leftovers. Do you stuff more food down your gullet just because it says, 'You're hungry, you old slob, get eating'? Remember, your mind can get mixed up.

MIND YOUR MIND

Treat your mind with respect. They don't do brain transplants yet, so you have to be kind to it! Your mind really is the marvel they all say it is, better than any computer around. Nevertheless, be careful about its limitations and its *modus operandi*. By itself, it cannot give you the vision to set up what you really want from life: it's not that type of instrument. You can't find a ship's position with a compass, for example; you use a sextant.

What reason does your mind give for wanting? You see a nice suit or dress: you want it. You spot a charming cottage: you want it. You hear there's work in a certain city: you want it. There are reduced fares to the Far East: you want a ticket. Your brother wants you over to see how well he's done abroad: you want to go. You go there: you want to emigrate!

Give your mind credit where it is due – it is looking after you in the best way it knows. When presented with a sequence of possibilities, it is indeed a wonder. For example, after a holiday somewhere, you decide you would like to live there. Perhaps you had a vague dissatisfaction with your former location, but this grows to total disgust, now you think you smell greener grass. In this case, your mind 'wants' what it thinks is best for you, then works with you to get the details sorted out. The ultimate process of moving to the new place is handled by the conscious, ever-so-logical mind. Finding ways of financing everything, selling up the old place, and establishing work at the new are all juggled and executed by the mind. These are the sort of tasks for which it is suited. But there is nothing to be gained by quickly writing up a list of wants, then posting it up the magic chimney of your mind. Your mind will agree with your list without question and try to arrange things without stopping to consider if they are practicable. So let's move on to more fruitful things. Bring your mind along. It's welcome. But keep your eye on it. It can be a tricky and unreliable piece of machinery!

WHAT IS SUCCESS FOR YOU?

At the outset, discover for yourself a means of *detaching the popular stereotypes of 'success' from what you feel to be right for you.* That is a sincere but loaded requisition. Do you really want a Porsche, or do you really hate driving altogether, no matter what image the wheels carry? Do you emphatically believe that success lies in a better job, or are you more realistically the type of person who could be in ecstasy on a low income, pottering at a lovely hobby you have? Do you feel that you are pushing yourself to make more and more friends, when you are actually happier with a small group of close confidantes? Please realize that pursuing false and artificial goals can precipitate excessive stress in our lives. Ideally, you should aim for the goals which cause 'creative' stress, not the chasing-your-tail stresses which debilitate. More will be said of this later (Chapters 9 and 10).

The future of success itself is interesting, and worth commenting upon right at the start. Popular models of success are slowly changing, so be aware of that. Money is becoming less central to the fabric of real success. (Ignore the clever people who gloat about turning over their shares or houses for a small fortune.) The successful people in the future might be those who:

- Are increasingly independent of all the usual constraints (job, mortgage, living on credit, gathering possessions just to be in the game).
- Desire wholeness rather than novelty, knowing that money does not buy happiness or fulfilment, but using it as leverage to create the things that do.
- Return to a simpler world view and enjoy modest pleasures such as growing flowers and taking music lessons rather than seeking oblivion from the present through the pleasure principle.
- Appreciate quality in everything: rather than buying shoddy (but trendy) mass-produced goods, they will seek well-made (even home-made) articles that last and can be repaired.
- Will be using their finite energies to change what they can instead of blaming everything on the government, banks, the stock market, the economy, recessions, parents, siblings, the weather, etc.

You are not a failure if you don't want a personal helicopter or a 10-bedroomed house. Trying to pursue goals that society or vanity specifies is absurd! What we perceive to be success and what we think we must do to get some of the action might both be mistakes from the start. Does success mean driving around your old neighbourhood in a Rolls-Royce, giving the neighbours the 'look-at-me' treatment? Is success jetting around on business, being interviewed by the top journals? You name what success is... But remember, there is no need to copy anyone else just because you're short of ideas yourself. You can be original with your success. Too many people are copy-cats. That, in a way, is cloning of the imagination. It is a waste of human talent and energy. Stand apart from the crowd and be your own person, with success to match!

When Jeff and Judy moved into their new house, they found most of their neighbours were like themselves – married one or two years with a child, one on the way, or thinking about it. It was a new development. The streets were still muddy from the builders. It was a new start for them after renting some dismal places. Their expectations were high.

They joined forces with the neighbours: building fences, moving soil about, buying materials together. That summer was tiring, but fun. Jeff and Judy became close through their labours, enjoying many pots of tea and shared laughter.

Their problems began with the parties. At first, they were simple affairs, an extension of the moving-in chumminess. But each party was slightly more grand than the last. The young couple survived the first round, but it wiped out their money for a tumble dryer. The second round was not so easy.

Then they fell in with Len and Phyllis, who dined out in style once a week. Jeff and Judy couldn't say no, so they dined with them. Dave next door convinced them they should have a better car; he had a friend in car sales. So they got a new car. It looked great in their drive. They signed up an expensive life insurance policy (that was Bill, two doors away). Then Mary suggested they join their group for a ski-ing holiday over the Christmas period. It was all very exciting, and they knew it was good to have really close neighbours who helped them all the time.

Within six months they were broke. Their bank account and the loan from Judy's father were history. The car was repossessed. When the furniture was lifted, their neighbours kept away. In fact, they haven't seen them since.

Now they live with Jeff's parents, but it's a squeeze. The house is sold again, to another nice young couple. Jeff and Judy walked past one evening, about 8.30. There was music from their house. A new car stood in the drive, with a ski-rack on the roof. Through the lace curtains, they noticed Bill explaining insurance numbers on his calculator; Len and Phyllis were explaining the tasting of wine. They walked on, reflecting how shallow it all seemed and how fragile the friendships were. It was so obvious now. They had been led along like trusting sheep, able to think for themselves, but unprepared to act alone.

APPLYING ENERGY TO THE RIGHT THINGS

The truth is, many people haven't a clue what they want, but they keep their minds actively 'wanting' all the while, unwittingly drawing disappointment upon themselves: 'I don't know specifically what I want, so I'll be miserable meanwhile!' In this state, the energy spent wanting is spread so thin that legitimate wants are seldom realized. If this energy were applied to one or two meaningful goals, with a vision of attainment, life might be less frustrating. That degree of focus is what you need to achieve goals of substance. It's similar to economists allocating 'scarce resources' to projects: there are always too few resources to go round, so the allocation must be focused, not diffuse.

You might not have much, but be thankful for it. Everything you have – whether it's a tank of tropical fish or the ability to make people laugh – be thankful for it. If you are miserable with what you have now, what logic says you are going to be a joyful person when you have possessions stacked to the roof? Many people have not progressed much beyond the example of the children in the toy department. It is fruitless to gather things around you in the vague hope that some synergy will occur, spawning instant happiness. Only if they are the right things will this occur. So focus on the right things, from this point onwards!

The young couple above did what was expected of them, and at the time, they had no idea what path they should have been on. We cannot glibly say they were silly to be led by others, and deserved to fall, for they acted in good faith at the time. How many young couples in the first flush of partnership sit down and draw up a life-map to follow? In Jeff and Judy's case, they were convinced they were making progress in the right place at the right time. (With so many sincere neighbours about them to help, of course.) But they had no final option but to withdraw from the dizzy race and return to reality, which essentially meant nothing more than living within their means.

It is a sad thing when we must withdraw in this way, because of external circumstances and not through conscious choice. But the lessons learned are valuable, if we can accept them graciously rather than with a feeling of devastation.

CHANGE AND ADAPTATION

Change is the best example of a universal truth we can honestly accept without much protest. You buy a house; you sell it. You get a job; you change it. You have a partner; you lose your partner. You buy shares; the prices go up. You place money in bonds; the rate plummets. Your friendly hairdresser quits; you have to adjust to the moody replacement. As change manifests itself in so many dimensions of our lives, our needs change. Our family is growing: we need a bigger house. The job is more demanding: we need a company car. Our job is lost: we need to cut expenses and scan the adverts.

When unexpected change arrives, though, we seldom consciously insist on choices that suit us personally. If, for example, we believe that by not accepting a promotion we won't ever be short-listed for good positions in the future, when promotion is offered, we will simply *do as we are told*, in effect. When we are offered such an opportunity, we can view it in three distinct ways:

God, this is awful, I'll hate this from the start, but it's a good leg up after all – I'll take it and the extra cash.
This is the very opportunity I've been dreaming of; I feel better already.
This is not for me. It will only set me back when I take my personal goals into account. It sounds like a good chance for someone, but not for me.

Which candidate are you? *Whatever* our judgement, we ought to have faith in it and stick to our resolution. If a prospect is really not for you, seek an alternative. If you feel you simply must take whatever is offered, you might end up getting something that appears worthwhile, but *did you originally want it?* This is the minimum-effort default position: 'I'll take what comes along.' Life is full of choices if you could but generate and exploit them, and there is no such thing as 'I must' when it comes to others (or your own vain mind) forcing you into default choices. Follow your nose, as they say. Real alternatives are your fundamental human rights. Don't say you are trapped – there are alternatives to every situation, if you but show a little patience.

Jake was new to the city, and he took an apartment near the river. One Saturday evening he put the supper on and strolled out to his balcony, 19 floors up.

Across the street, and on the other side of an open parking area, stood the twin towers of the trendiest place to have an apartment. He noticed a lovely girl leaning on the railing, perhaps 22 floors up. She was looking around and studying the taxi-cabs and night traffic on the way to good times. Jake wished at that moment she could be with him to share his steak and onions, but realized she was totally unaware of him.

As he sat down to his supper, the noise of the city streamed in through his open patio-door. Police cars were chasing around, sirens blooping on and off. One siren had stopped somewhere down below. A fire truck maybe. People living in high-rise apartments always check out where the fire truck stops...

It wasn't a fire truck, but an ambulance and two police cars. Jake picked out a red blanket on the street, then the form of a person. A pedestrian hit by a car, he supposed. He looked up at the apartment opposite. People stood there, spectating from their balconies. He wondered why the girl wasn't there, because her patio-door was open. Then it all clicked.

They took away the red blanket and put sand down. The ambulance pulled away; the siren was not used.

It made no news. Jake found out the details from a friend at work who was staying in the same apartment block. She had broken up with her boyfriend of two months, because he was going to college. She was 20 years old and facing a confusing, critical Saturday night in a big city, with absolutely no alternatives.

FROM THE MUNDANE TO THE EXCELLENT

Are you a special person, or are you ordinary? Let's play risky and say you are extra special. That does not mean you are *better*, of course. That is a subjective game of nonsense. Now when you believe that you are special, you will help others to realize they might be special too.

Every special person has special needs. Special people have very special ideas of what they're here for, and what they're going to make of it all. They can say, 'I know who I am, what I'm here for, and where I've yet to go.' They assimilate with their own unique properties and latent potential. They understand and learn to have control over what is going on, rather than blindly accepting what is presented to them. By understanding themselves well, and appreciating how this funny old world continues to carry on every day (against all the odds), they discover things about life they once thought must be secret. These are the secrets kept hidden from mankind by mankind.

Special people learn how to identify and align themselves with the things they want. They refuse to model every thinking moment on other people's lives, or the complications thereof. They refuse to compare what they have or do not have with neighbours, friends or characters in the media (or fantasy). Special people refuse to forfeit their hard-won contentment and peace of mind when put under pressure from the fanatical ideas of others. They refuse to allow conflict between their inner satisfaction and the popular consensus about forever wanting more and expecting it to come like manna from heaven. You too are a special person – yes, you are! So think and act like one, with the world under your feet, where it should be!

NO SIMPLE 'WANTING FORMULA'

Your personal wants might appear very straightforward to some people. Perhaps you want nothing – or perhaps you want a chain of international hotels around the world and a personal jet to visit them with. Don't feel guilty either way. You are absolutely on target, *if that is what you want!* Your wants can seldom be too simple or too outrageous. Providence is not going to punish you for appearing greedy. If you set out to get what you want honestly, and it is precisely what you have dedicated your wishes to, then you will actually get support from Providence! Disbelieve this at your peril. You know you don't have all the answers; that's why you're reading this book — to get some of them!

Jean sent the coupon away, with her choices in order: DGFACEB. She wasn't sure if floor organization was better than piped music, but that was her choice.

When the letter arrived, she nearly threw it in her coupon box on top of the fridge. Opening it, she discovered she had won first prize: five minutes of fully paid shopping in a giant supermarket.

She picked a Wednesday morning for the spree. The manager welcomed her, and a television crew was there to follow the event.

After some preliminaries, the clock was started. Jean sped off down the first aisle with the multitude trying to keep up. They couldn't catch her, but a full minute before the timer went off, she appeared at checkout 16 with a trolley loaded like a ten-armed man at a looting. Within seconds, everyone was crowded around, with the TV camera shooting it all.

'I always wanted the very best, but I couldn't afford it. And I hate the carrying. This'll keep me going for my lifetime,' she said.

Piled on the trolley, like neatly-laid bricks in a master-mason's wall, were 400 best quality toilet rolls, absolutely top-of-the-line and undoubtedly used by the very best.

PREFERENCES

Take your notebook and venture a little further! This exercise will help to highlight your *present* tastes. Avoid any structuring: allow free association of ideas. Simply write down your likes and dislikes, using the format responses as a prompt.

LIKES	REASONS
Cheerful people.	Being serious is boring.
Learning new things.	It keeps my mind active.
Relaxed times with best friends.	I feel safe, that I *belong*.
Non-competitive sports.	Winning isn't important.

DISLIKES	REASONS
Waiting in queues.	I suppose I'm impatient.
People that put me down.	I'm as good as anyone.
Limitations of my present job.	Earnings and prospects poor.
Meeting new people.	It takes so much effort.

PICKING UP THE THREAD

How would you describe this person? Selective, especially with people, with a vague desire to be successful but a lack of interest in applying effort...? Someone wishing the right 'luck' to come along but unable or afraid to accept the responsibility of taking an active part in trying alternatives? Is this you? Looking at your own Preferences worksheet, how would you describe yourself? Sometimes the little things suggest significant patterns of alignment, a common thread. You might discover your own dislikes fill the page: now that might tell you something!

When it comes to applying the outcome of Preferences, that is, using your present tastes to determine your wants, remember that listening to your mind's constant chattering will give you nothing but a jumble. So we need to explore further.

PAPER AND PENCIL – AGAIN!

The cheapest and most functional exploration method requires a pad of paper, a pencil, an eraser, a selection of coloured pencils and a comfortable, quiet place to sit. You'll need a table or a desk, or if a good clipboard is more your style, OK, great! But sitting in an arm-chair with a drink, snacks, and the television on is not the way. So get to it and organize yourself for a little effort!

Do you know how to 'open up' on paper? You can learn to use both written and visual techniques to communicate with yourself. Sitting thinking about your ideas is next to useless, because your mind has no focus of its own. And a mind without focus is like a slide show with the projector lens missing. So don't make things difficult for yourself.

To work out your ideas, write down your thoughts, fears, frustra-tions, dreams and problems, or draw little cartoons or symbols that give you a visual image of how things really are, or how they might be. If you think you're a failure and the world's against you, write all your negative words down. If you feel frustrated in your work, draw a little person behind steel mesh shouting 'HELP!' If your mind keeps focusing on exploring the world, draw a montage of places you want to visit, with an airliner parachuting you in! When you see your dreams on paper, you'll begin to realize that perhaps there's still hope of realizing them. It's good fun. I call it 'note-pad prayer': getting to know yourself, 'talking to yourself' in your own everyday words – four-letter ones too if it helps!

DRAWING UP A 'WANT MAP'

Together we are going to construct a map of your present position and the possibilities open to you. This exercise will cover all the things that matter at this point. (You may want to adjust the exercise to your own special needs once you see how it works.) The first stage is to prepare three tables of notes. The objective of this is to get you in touch with yourself, and to help you *extend yourself in the ways you choose*. What you want will hopefully become clear to you as the process develops. If you try to by-pass this first part of the exercise and go straight on to deciding what you want, you'll miss the point. The aim is to determine what is right for you, not just end up with a string of things that seem better than what you presently have.

Begin by referring to the material and personal inventories you prepared earlier. These exercises helped you to see where you stood in a relatively quantitative way. Now you will extend these findings into a series of 'paper dialogues'.

In this exercise there are three 'levels' of exploration: Facts, Feelings and Wants. Each level has a set of common headings to build a more comprehensive picture. These headings are:

Circumstances
Finances
Career
Personal
Relationships
Consciousness

Starting with Facts, write down everything about your present position. Apply the principle of free association of ideas. Don't miss out anything important, even if it doesn't seem to fit any of the categories directly, and keep focused on the task at hand. Take one step at a time, or you'll end up with an electrical storm in your head. If your job is uncertain, say so; if your bank account is low, state how low.

Similarly, if you find that you quarrel with people at work, then that's a fact too, to be listed under Relationships. There is an example of a completed set of notes below, to help you.

The next level, Feelings, requires more attention. How do you *feel* about your circumstances, your finances, your career situation? Are you content with the situation, or troubled by specific problems? Explore your feelings under each heading. Put the words in your own language; there's no need to be formal.

The third level, Wants, comes to terms with Facts and Feelings, and looks to the future. Given the facts, and then understanding your feelings towards them, *what could happen to improve things?* Don't ask how at this point. If your job is uncertain (*fact*) and you *feel* terrible about that, what do you *want* to brighten up your picture? If you get totally stuck, try the exercise again, but starting with Wants. Simply declare what you *want* up front, then proceed backwards to reality (your facts and feelings). I know it defies logic, but professional problem-solving techniques use this approach to break through blockages! Have fun with this exercise. You'll learn a lot about yourself, and what you want from life will become progressively clearer, I promise you!

The example provided here is built up around a fictitious soul with a realistic situation. Monetary amounts are quoted in 'universal units' to avoid a subliminal benchmark! Again, use the method, not the similarities. You will be starting with blank pages and your own situation.

Level I: Facts
Circumstances

Living in a two-bedroomed house with my wife and daughter. Heavy commitments to family and various debts. Job a bit uncertain in the long term (recent layoff). Wife pregnant. Relatives arriving for holiday this summer. Trying to help brother-in-law find a job in this area.

Finances

House value: 74,000. Mortgage: 58,000. Equity: 16,000.

Bank account: 7,400.

Bank loan for car: 3,200 still outstanding.

Possessions, estimated value: 2,600. Car: 3,400.

Present salary: 10,200 pa.

Career

Work unstable since recent take-over. Some layoffs already.

New boss difficult to work with.

Generally satisfied with work, but company has changed.

Wife finished part-time work due to baby.

My skills are difficult to apply in other work.

Personal

I can't make decisions any more. I can't concentrate.

I have trouble trusting people now. I look for their faults.

I lose my cool often and let people know what I think.

Recently, I'm tired all the time, lazy and careless.

I'm impatient, ultra-sensitive and lacking daily confidence.

Relationships

Wife is becoming moody and dissatisfied with our lot.

I have quarrels with people at work.

I've lost my faith in people I formerly trusted.

I'm tired of seeing my friends at social events.

Consciousness

Sometimes I'm 'observing' myself, watching my stupid behaviour.

I think people see that I'm not too bright these days.

I have a sense of impending failure when I think too much.

I borrow books on psychology from the local library!

Level II: Feelings

Circumstances

I wanted a decent salary after working in my home town, so we moved here. But the mortgage is frightening, with another child on the way. And this damned job! Will I be the next one to get the boot? I wish our relatives would leave the holiday till we get on our feet here. And Linda's brother isn't worth finding a job for!

Finances

On paper I'm worth about 20,000 clear. My salary is OK but it could be higher. Back home on this salary I'd feel well-off. But if I lose my job here, the whole thing falls apart, and that worries me. The roof and chimney need maintenance. We're saving nothing now that Linda's stopped work.

Career

I'm wary of this firm, especially after the take-over. Sooner or later I'll quit on the spot, because of that clown they put over me. I know all about plastic insulators for electrical appliances, but who else would need that? I've painted myself into a corner this time.

Personal

I think I'm falling apart every day. I nearly slapped my daughter yesterday, something I swore I'd never do. Every time I try to see a better way, I lose interest and want to sleep in a chair. I just feel I've reached the point of no solutions. I can't think straight. I'm under stress.

Relationships

My poor wife! I lie in bed thinking what stupid things I said to her, and I feel remorse to the core. But do I learn? I give her nothing but bickering the next day. My friends seem distant to me. To be honest, I don't have a close friend just now. That's a bad sign!

Consciousness

I'm conscious of being in trouble, or at least out of control. Maybe work isn't altogether to blame. After all, it's not everything. I have nothing substantial to hang onto. Well, my wife, yes, but she thinks I'm on the way down or something. She doesn't say much. The idea of slipping into depression crossed my mind.

Level III: Wants

Circumstances

We like our house. With two children it will do until an extension could be added. Other people have high mortgages; ours isn't too ridiculous. We'll make it clear that our guests pay their way. Tell Linda's brother to get down here and look for jobs himself!

Finances

We're not that badly placed after a year here. If we had to move, we have enough to manage. The roof hasn't leaked yet, so we can defer that job. Although we must have more income with another mouth to feed soon.

Career

I'll start thinking about other jobs that I could use my skills in. Electrical insulators must be used in other things. Maybe catalogues would get me thinking. There's no doubt, I'm not happy with this company any more. I'll wait a month or two and ask for a decent salary increase. Meanwhile, I'll look around.

Personal

My behaviour has to improve, otherwise I'll lose my job whether I want to or not, and my wife will leave me. It's time I developed new interests; I'm going quite stale. I'm tired of my leisure activities. Perhaps my priorities have changed, so I'll look for a new stimulus. No more sitting in chairs and snoozing either!

Relationships

I have to discuss the problems with my wife, rather than brooding about them myself. She keeps quiet because she's becoming scared of me! Imagine! I should think about making friends through some new activity, like joining a tennis club. I must find some close friends. How about my wife, for one?

Consciousness

There's something wrong all right. That's the easy part. I must see it as it is, and take steps to get out of this hole. I'm more miserable than I need be: even I can admit to that. But once we get things under way in the next few months, it will all fall into place. Why should I punish myself and everyone around me?

Now you have come this far, you can try to summarize your current situation – facts, feelings and wants. What does it reveal about yourself?

FROM 'WANTS' TO 'GOALS'

Stretching for what we would really like, beyond what we have to get along with, is the next step in the proceedings. The case study above, designed to help you in your search, was a typical 'crisis' situation.

Quite often, growth does begin with a crisis situation. The crisis is either forced on you by external circumstances, or you must artificially induce a crisis to make the process real and shake yourself from apathy. Welcoming this state of crisis should be interpreted as 'creating a climate of desirable stress' (see Chapters 9 and 10). Without a healthy pinch of stress, a sense of urgency if you like, the wheels will fail to spin into motion. If you allow yourself to be overcome by apathy, then all the exercises you do will be wasted. But if you risk a little, and rattle your cage with a big stick, you will rise to the occasion and do very well!

Level IV, the goal zone, is the next band of exploration. Once your wants have been defined, what is beyond that? You can start taking bolder steps now! For instance, our friend in the example has rightly reassured himself he has skills that another company could use – even after the destructive anguish of his self-doubt. If he developed some other skills, either by planned training or personal redirection, could he become a salesman of plastic mouldings or even start his own company, specializing in the most sophisticated and profitable components?

Remember, you will never have the nerve to contemplate Level IV if you decide you are 'destined' to stay at Level II or III. So many people consciously *choose* to agonize over their bad fortune. But worrying guarantees a muddled head, and drains vital energy away into a bottomless pit. That is why you must methodically work through this exercise, for each stage will lead to a higher level of clear perspectives and possibilities, and your confidence will grow accordingly. Go forward with that emerging confidence and think about the waiting potential in Level IV!

NOTHING TO FEAR BUT FEAR

Look back on your life for a moment. How many of the worries, fears and terrors that you anguished over came to pass? Was your house repossessed when the mortgage rate went up? Did the big end bearings fail on your old car as you expected them to? Did your teenage daughter run off with a cult after all? Was that abdominal pain what you thought it might be at first? Worry pens us in, overwhelms us, makes us weak, rattles our knee-joints. It causes butterflies in the stomach and snakes in the intestines. It is the essence of psychosomatic-related disorders such as ulcers, strokes, cancer and digestive problems.

In any worrying situation, assess what the *worst possible* outcome could be. Assume that the worst would happen. Would it necessarily ruin you? Could you see ways to deal with it, whatever it might be? You will notice that honesty and resignation to the situation will generate solutions – and worrying is an extra burden you can dispense with altogether. In deciding what you may want from life, dispense with worry. Say 'Enough!' Worry will only set boundaries and conditions on your skill to navigate through the fog.

There is today, and there is tomorrow. A state of equilibrium which makes sense of both *can* be achieved in your life. What is best for you will suggest itself, by intuition more than reason, whether it's running your own company or having a lifetime's supply of toilet rolls. Use your focused mind to flesh out the things you want. *Beware of the unfocused, chattering mind of 'I want, I want, I want.'* Setting goals will then be lots of fun for you. Later I'll explain how you're going to see them come true.

This has been a warm-up session to make you think about yourself and your future in a logical way. It may have helped to clarify what you should be doing with your life, but please don't expect conclusive insights this early. Stay interested, though, and become even more motivated! You are making great progress through some exacting work! Next on the agenda: some insights and warnings about the ways we become overwhelmed by external events and the hands of fate. I'll show you how to cross boundaries there too!

REVIEW

1 You have learned how to 'want' creatively – no more vague and muddled desires which fail the test of time!
2 Understanding the chaotic and arbitrary nature of your mind has forced you to think with purpose, not with hollow cravings.
3 The nature and value of person-specific success has become clear to you.
4 By following a structured exercise, you have explored your situation more intimately and discovered exciting possibilities for further attention.

7 Upwaves, Downwaves

To prophesy is extremely difficult, especially with respect to the future.

Chinese Proverb

OVERVIEW

Are we controlled by pre-ordained fate, or do we have free will to choose our futures? Is the world really as terrible as they say it is? Are the odds stacked against us, making ambition rather futile? If this is our world view, the only respite may be to blame someone or something!

We do have control, we can make choices – and the Open Person has a distinct advantage. We can choose to think independently of 'the system' and rely on inner awareness rather than external data.

Life is not a haphazard process subject to external events, with people losing ground rather than winning. We are not compelled by the world, but free to make constructive choices and act as unique individuals.

THE INSECURITY BLOCKAGE

Our individual, unique perception of events and experiences can be a measure of our own insecurity. Every one of us sees this world differently. To some, the world is a living hell – and they don't have to be living in the world's trouble-spots. Others endure testing circumstances every day, but seem to float along on a joyful cloud, seeing wonder and beauty everywhere. Which person is more in touch with reality?

We are inundated with information on the state of the world, and it is difficult to deny that it affects us. The external world is there all right, but must we be intimidated by it? Start watching the television news regularly every evening, and you will realize how often we dwell on the *negative* aspects of life. They seldom (if ever) identify the things they want because they are forever whining about the weather, interest rates, the price of butter . . . or the inherent unfairness of life! I'm sure that you catch yourself stuck in this mode sometimes, at least on the bad days. But it doesn't help much, does it?

In everyday speech and behaviour, appearing positive has become distasteful and embarrassing for many people. Praise, compliments, politeness, respect, encouragement – these are treated with *suspicion*! Focusing on the negative has, for many people, become a way of life, a process of 'automatic thinking' where the herd instinct rules. Perhaps the underlying problem is insecurity. By conforming to a lower common denominator (a largely negative outlook), there is *no need to try too hard* ('Everything's so *difficult*, isn't it?') And there's safety in numbers ('Yes, we all agree, the world is a mess, and talking about it seems to pass the time.') Going forth with a spring in your step and a positive outlook might invite criticism and offend people! But that's the sort of 'unsocial' behaviour I'm asking of you. If you have succumbed to society's negative clutches, I'm going to give you a shake!

OVERWHELMED BY EXTERNAL EVENTS?

All news affects you. *Try ignoring all sources of news or media discussion for two weeks,* and consciously move away from others who are debating the current tragedies, horrors or intrigues. You may invite criticism from the 'information die-hards' for tuning out society's troubles, but try it for a while.

People keep themselves informed of the world's problems as a *partial purpose to life.* As a rule, we are urged to take heed and believe that the experts are always right because they have more *data* than us. Then the doom-peddlers pass the gloomy consensus down to us, like a gift. A shift of guilt occurs. Together, we create a dubious new moral philosophy based on miserable people, all wrapped up in current affairs!

Some say we become what we eat. That may not be as accurate as what we become through stuffing ourselves with information that we did not create ourselves. We can refuse food we can't abide, or our stomachs will reject it for us. But how do we handle the banquet of information pressed on us daily? We seek out information like vital sustenance, craving it and thriving on it. 'Quiet, everyone, the news is on!'

A COG ON A WHEEL?

The individual person is seen by many these days purely as an economic unit. We are linked in to interest rates, housing costs, salary levels, the cost-of-living index, inflation, and credit risks, to name but a few. The life of the world and all who tread on it is fuelled by political factors, by debt, recessions, booms, crises, competition, technology changes and good old fate. A bad session in one stock market affects another market in a different time zone within a matter of hours. Interest rates may move, mortgage payments change, the reduced money supply may mean restricted borrowing and company lay-offs – we are all caught up in the big global cycles, or at least that's what they're shouting at us! Some are winning, some losing. Who can we believe any more? What exactly controls the whole thing, and where do I fit into that? Fear and confusion are inevitable when too many negative facts are fired at us. Then comes the surrender of the will, the fear to act at all. We believe that *other people* are understanding the system – that's why they're successful – but lack confidence in our own judgement.

My house is losing value, while others are retiring at 50 on their profits. My small business went bust in a year. That man up the street is employing four more people this week. It's this damned world recession. When's it going to end? Every time I have a good idea, there's a world recession! They say things are getting better after the last trade figures – order books filling up, new opportunities everywhere. So why can't I find a job? Everyone's lying. The news is full of useless facts that can't help me, and I don't know where to look any more.

Too many people see things this way. Our modern society seems to be obsessed by numerate definitions of everything. The individual is treated as a resource and a consumer, and when someone ceases to be resourceful, or fails to be a model consumer, he or she is perceived to be anti-social or to have less value. But be that as it may, you and I, as Open People, need not see ourselves like this at all! This might appear too simplistic, but we really *can* detach ourselves from the gloomy consensus. If we refuse to be automatic thinkers (non-thinkers?), we can decide to find alternatives – positive, constructive alternatives! But we must fully appreciate the negative, the downwave forces so we know what we have to overcome.

THE ESCAPIST POLITICS OF BLAME

Finding someone or something to blame is great fun. You have so many choices. Several bricks have gone through television screens for this very reason! People like to blame the system, society, the banks, big business, politicians and God. Blaming God is especially popular when the going is really tough. We can imagine Him heaping on the problems, testing us, warning us, punishing us. It's a nice theory, but quite wrong. God neither imposes the problems, nor solves them. But He does care about our many predicaments, crises, episodes of anguish and pain. Knowing that gives us strength to cope. We would all like a perfect world, with perfect lives and no downwaves, ever. So since we live in a real world, we look for guilty parties:

My parents are to blame for the way I've turned out. My father lived in his own world of keeping other people's books and pretending he was a Chartered Accountant. His idea of excitement was a Rotary Club meeting once in a blue moon. Mother was always in the house, the garden, or in shops. I can't think of where else she spent any significant time, apart from visiting an elderly friend on Thursday afternoons.

They gave me what could be expected, I suppose. We got along, in a fashion. But, really, we hardly knew each other.

When I left home, I went a bit wild. It was the feeling of freedom. My first year at university was great, but I failed all but one subject. I dropped out and went to work as a dishwasher in a resort hotel. From then on, I had jobs here, jobs there. I can't say I've been in any place for more than a year. Recently I had a serious accident coming home from a party with a car I borrowed. I wasn't badly hurt, but the other fellow was. The whole thing's like a punishment.

I get these notions about starting again, but that's impossible with my background. If only I had parents with some contacts, instead of a dreary pair of lower middle-class bores. They didn't start me off right in the first place. How could they? They were lost in a deeper rut than me, and I hate them for it.

This young man is very effective in passing the blame to others, and does it with great energy and enthusiasm. In a sense, he is probably right. A father estranged from his son, by reason of his simple lifestyle. A mother who was 'just a housewife'. Yet what problems did the father have? Was he ashamed of his status, pretending he was a real accountant? Did the Rotary Club meetings give him a sense of belonging or identity that his son never gave to him? And what exactly were his mother's motives in visiting an elderly person? Perhaps she was having a superb time sharing funny stories with a lively old soul, whereas she had to endure two uncaring males at home. Parents are humans, real people, too. They are just as likely to be confused or in a mess with their lives. At the very least, they don't have access to all the answers just because they are parents.

To go back to the son, he lived his *own* life in the big wide world and it turned out to be a failure. But he still believes it is his parents' fault that life is unfair. If he keeps on this way, he will soon be able to sign over his life to counsellors and psychologists, for he is always searching for the answers from someone else.

FROM BLAME TO UNDERSTANDING

Many difficult and unfair situations do have blame components in them. Wicked people causing unpleasant or damaging circumstances is one example – if they were to act in a different and more compassionate way, many miseries could be avoided. Yet everyone is *free to act as they will*, and through lack of judgement, or sheer callousness, hurtful events are born. Fingers can be pointed, but *how long* can you hold your arm up in anger? Instead of finding others to blame, move on swiftly to the immediate problem: *yourself*. Stop seeing yourself as persecuted, betrayed, unlucky, unjustly wronged, a failure, as someone who will never achieve anything worthwhile because of others or the past. *See yourself as unique, gifted, resourceful, innovative, motivated and very lucky!* Now isn't that a lovely sprinkle of positive words after all those negatives? Feel any better?

What you do have control over is your freedom. But how on Earth, you might ask, could you have freedom in a world so structured and controlled? How can it be, when the system is so tightly strung that a one per cent rise in interest rates destroys thousands of small businesses? But what you do have, whether you see it as responsible or not, is *the freedom to opt out*. You can choose to think freely and effectively, without all the noise and turbulence of the system. Just as you could survive without television for two weeks, so you can make it without untiring homage to 'the system'.

Once you can grasp the reality of being in the world, *but not necessarily compelled by it*, you can make some progress. There is no need to drop out of society and go to the nearest commune just to think. Some have tried living in monasteries or other inspirational centres, and if that is what you feel you should do, fine. However, most people will opt to start thinking independently, and sort themselves out, while still paying the mortgage and the milkman.

What you need is to determine where you are, relative to the noise out there. Your illusions or your theories about the world will have to be put into hibernation for a while. There's no need to laugh at tragedy when you hear of it, nor ignore the reminders on your outstanding electric bill, just realize that you must *rise above* the fuss and the facts. There are certainly upwaves and downwaves: stock market bulls and bears; low interest rates, high interest rates; inflation, deflation, stagnation. These things will continue to happen. But you are neither a subject of the Big Boys nor a pawn in their game – unless you believe you are. *Stand apart: find that precious centre of integrity and self-worth in yourself, and thoroughly believe in it.*

We tend to follow the crowd because it is easy. Shaking off cosy illusions is painful; standing apart, lonely. We have collective beliefs, seldom our own. When fate deals us a cruel blow, we feel it is not due to the normal processes of life and reality, but a personal kick in the shins from the system. When times go well, we think we have been clever and have done all the right things. It is fun to prove our life-theories to ourselves. After all, we like to believe they give life meaning. How do you see yourself against these popular beliefs? No doubt you will identify areas of your thinking which may require work. Test your attitudes as you go. Throw the bad ones out, like weeding an untidy garden.

ILLUSIONS IN THE WORLD OF WORK

The world of employment is a good source of insight into the workings of fate. Employment gives us a personal stake in the upwave/downwave game. However the company is doing affects us. We want our organization to do well, because that will give us more security and a chance of career growth. By grooming ourselves in what we do, we hope to enjoy constantly increasing expectations, a better fate.

Our ideas of work, wages, effort and ambition are also loosely related to the larger world picture of achieving 'progress'. That progress is interpreted as our personal upwave, should we be on the winning end. If you are prospering in the Information Technology sector, recession is a relative term for you. A dairy farmer facing bank foreclosures and ruin, though, can only see himself on a downwave, and may end up cursing the government, the banks – and maybe even his parents!

Work has achieved a very high profile in our perception of the world. At election time, people interviewed in the street usually blame the government for not doing anything about unemployment, whether they are in areas of high unemployment or not. Are our lives nothing without work? Are they really so one-dimensional? For many people, work is their only point of focus in contemplating upwaves and downwaves. Work makes their lives; lack of it destroys them. A job can be a substitute for the meaning of life. Career building is often a demonstration of self-projection, ego and vanity. Men are particularly bound up in the ladders (and snakes) of status, competition and outward success, and the demands are infinite on the willing. Women in the career game are no less misled. For employment is not ultimate truth, it is simply hiring your time out for a price. Work gives us something to build illusions on. We like to think it protects us from tragedies – well, it does, some of the time.

Janine was sketching something at her desk, unaware of the time, but conscious that the coffee had not passed. It was quiet in the office today. She wandered over to see what Tessa might be sticking on her paste-up boards.

The group stood behind a row of cabinets, talking quietly.

'Well, that's the drawing office wiped out,' one said.

As the day wore on, people were receiving phone calls like breaths from the Grim Reaper, but the phone beside Janine was silent. A single selfish thought shocked her: I'm still in, they didn't pick me, I'm of value here! There was a fundamental difference between people in this world, she reasoned. Some lose, others don't. Survival of the fittest. She was happy about that. It's human, of course, to feel sorry at the time – so her soul was still in the right place. Anyway, she'd never see those people again, most likely.

Business returned to normal, and the remaining staff regrouped quickly. Things looked brighter. Janine went home one Friday to fry trout and maybe open a bottle of supermarket wine. She felt good, content. The phone rang while the fish crackled in the pan. It was a simple message, and she understood it easily: 'Your position is terminated, effective immediately; a letter will be sent to you with the details.'

'Always the other person until it's me' – we know the feeling. When the other person loses the dash against fate and is swallowed up, we feel that odd flush of embarrassed relief. Not me! They deserved it maybe, it's their karma, or their wickedness being redressed by God, fair and square. We smugly assume that somehow the world makes sense; it's not all haphazard chaos and chance. Yet when dreaded phone calls or letters do afflict us, it's an entirely different world. Out come the torrents of blame, the theories on justice, the world view of bitter cynicism, anger and hurt. Yet we cannot build futures on bitterness. Easy to write, to read, you say, but difficult to implement. Nevertheless, if we are to make the best of our lives, the question is not why but what now?

The moment we think we understand the facts, theories, cycles, rules or patterns, we are abruptly reminded that all our illusions are more notional than sensible. All of them! We may have studied the news, the facts, logic and trends, taken courses to prepare for better things, had watertight personal philosophies of how rewards were allocated, punishments inflicted... Then fate descends on us out of the blue and burns the trout! Does fate have the final word?

Dealing with fate is a process of letting go, accepting what is, refusing to cling to facts, theories, illusions, angry battles over justice. But then, people often delight in avoiding reality. Are you tempted to avoid reality sometimes? Can you see that there are no guarantees on our tomorrows, that excessive fear is counter-productive, that fate is mostly a phantom of the mind?

DATA OVERLOAD AND THE INDEPENDENT MIND

It is a true fact that educated, intellectual and well-informed people often fail miserably in entrepreneurial ventures. While they are studying some trend or other, they lose an order to their competitor who works out of a garden shed and has only one qualification, in arithmetic. Experts often have little imagination – stuffed with facts and theories, they are generally fearful about every step they take.

True thinkers, on the other hand, have humble but open minds. They are honest with themselves, and admit they haven't a clue when faced with information on all fronts. Their strength lies in facing problems squarely, making decisions and making them quickly. (Isn't that what everyday life is all about too?) Making the wrong decisions doesn't trouble them at all. They press on and enjoy being different, right or wrong. As they experience the hard realities of their decisions, they grow smart and learn how to be right more often. On the other hand, perfectionists can talk about the problems for hours, but defer the move towards solutions.

LIFE IS MAKING DECISIONS

How can we discover how to make the right decisions? Or how to make decisions at all? We can learn something here from the business world. Decision-making in large business organizations can sometimes be an interesting study in brilliant procrastination. Corporate decision-making is normally based on some accepted rules of order:

Terms of reference (chairman's ideas, concerns).
Defining the problem or the need for change.
Interviews and discussion sessions.
Fact analysis and classification.
Generation and evaluation of alternatives.
Presentation of findings with reasoning.

With complex issues involving resources of people, capital and physical facilities, this process is essentially rational. It is especially relevant for production, financial, marketing and distribution operations. When applied to less tangible problems, however, the results suffer the consequences of trying to put everything through the same machine.

Even with all the best brains assembled, using the most sophisticated business tools, blunders are still made. When we trust facts or computers or experts or consultants to make our decisions for us, we are often kidding ourselves. Of course, when a decision goes wrong, we can then blame the computer! We might even find a way to blame our parents, or God, or the price of molasses on the commodities market! But it would be better to spend the time understanding how lost we make ourselves by relying on all those personal distortions and external things. Blaming others, or the system, wastes precious energy. And if we fall in love with reason, it will only lead us into more 'educated confusion'.

SO HOW WILL YOU DECIDE?

There are no upwaves or downwaves in the world you can choose to see. Only you, today and tomorrow. Listen to yourself for a change; switch off the experts. They can take up such a lot of your time, and absorb your energy. Once you learn to live beyond their 'help', you can watch and read for contrast, not direction. The world is not as finite or as fatalistic as you might think. Don't waste your life waiting for the next upwave – it might arrive too late for you to even see it!

Furthermore, living life as a process of good and bad luck, waiting for the winds to reverse, is also likely to be frustrating. One of the basic rules of life is that *fairness may not be possible*. Another rule, however, is that we always have the power to act, to make choices, and to do so cheerfully, even when we'd like to scream!

All that Open Person training should be paying off now. You will begin to see external events and the upwave/downwave cycles in a more enlightened way. The concept of *self-destiny* is meaningful to the Open Person. Quite simply, destiny lies in your hands, and you know it! At last you can rise above people defining you as an economic unit or a statistic! Your integrity and independent air will make you free to choose, free to make your own way. Even if life throws up some unexpected or unpleasant surprises, you will be better prepared to cope.

This self-development business really boils down to making your own decisions, and learning how to get them right as often as possible. You are becoming a problem-solving unit, a powerful decision-maker! You know now that too much data only leads to distraction and confusion. Similarly, too much attention to negative commentaries makes progress look impossible. But above all, you now understand that *your attitude* sets the stage for the future, not the stock market or vague scapegoats like unsupportive parents or sibling rivalry. With these winning ideas in your open mind, you are now ready to write some very positive goals!

REVIEW

1 You have recognized that (despite the negative press) life is still worth living to the full.
2 Any defeatist attitudes on the 'unfairness' of life have evaporated around you.
3 You have taken responsibility for your situation, rather than scapegoating or becoming miserable through apathy!
4 Change is part of the life process: you have learned to accept change (good or bad) and adapt to it with resolve, not self-pity or frustration.

PART 3
What Are Your Goals and How Will You Achieve Them?

FORWARD PASSAGE...
FROM NEGATIVE...   **TO POSITIVE**

'It all sounds so simple, but life just isn't like that. I know.'

'I'm learning every day, and life can have pleasant surprises.'

'Yes I could be a better person, more prosperous too. But every time I try, the next hurdle knocks me down.'

'Life's challenges do present difficulties, but I pick myself up and try again.'

'I tried thinking positive once. People thought I was soft in the head.'

'Positive thinking might be the label; I just call it setting goals and managing my life.'

'My attitudes might be wrong, but success isn't my destiny, whether I change or not.'

'Success is always available to me; I can arrange it through goals and focused effort.'

'I have enough stress in my life without piling on more demands.'

'I am aware of stress but unafraid of it, given some understanding.'

'Playing with your mind is weird. It frightens me.'

'My mind is the essence of my consciousness. Understanding it will open doors.'

8 Setting Goals: Why Not?

The secret of success is constancy to purpose.

Benjamin Disraeli

> **OVERVIEW**
>
> Now that we have studied certain preliminaries, the exciting process of setting goals is next on the agenda. We are sometimes inhibited about declaring goals, but now is the time to turn vague wishes into concrete objectives. Earlier discussion has identified where you are, and where you would like to be. Goals focus wishes and activate energies which will convert them from paper plans to action plans.
>
> Personal and material goals are developed through a 'reasoning' process which starts with an internal dialogue. A goal is a *positive affirmation* – the desired outcome stated as if it were already accomplished.
>
> The concept of visualization (seeing the finished goals) is introduced in this chapter. Emphasis is placed on the 'mind's eye' view of the future (self-suggestion).

ARE YOU THE GOAL TYPE?

You might not like the term 'goals'. Perhaps it's an unfortunate word for you. The word 'goals' has unhappily become associated with career-hungry executives and greedy people building their self-centred Utopias. You might consider another word, such as 'ambitions', 'choices', 'desires', 'wishes', 'aspirations', 'aims', 'directions', 'endeavours' or 'purposes'. Choose whatever word suits you, or stick with 'goals' for convenience.

Some false aesthetics have been built up over the years about goals, with various schools of positive thinking and management grooming driving the practice of setting goals almost to exhaustion. We mainly associate goals with a business context and not with personal use. There has been a competitive allusion too. Employers at staff interviews glibly ask about five-year goals, or next year's targets. Are we caught up in a Wonderland game of croquet, where we lose our heads if we can't score? 'Give me one negative thought, and there's no jam for you today!'

In fact, a complete jargon has arisen over the years in the business of getting you to better yourself. There has to be a 'game plan', an 'action list', a 'critical path' to somewhere, together with some sort of 'performance indicators' or 'criteria', and maybe a set of 'functional parameters'. Impressive words! It is time to begin a new and less esoteric set of terms. How about 'I'm lost', 'I could be in a rut', 'I need help' and 'I think I can find a way forward'? Don't ever be intimidated by the unintelligible terms and catch-phrases in 'successful thinking' or self-development literature! Just make sure you are comfortable with your own ideas and feelings, and what you are trying to do.

Approach your goal definition with enthusiasm, and do it cheerfully. If you treat it as an exercise in futility, you choose to remain where you are. You are responsible for what you do, so do it well. And do it on your own. Allow your partner or your friends into this programme and you might not hear your own vital whispers for their babble. All you need is a classical skeptic or a well-meaning comedian to reduce your goals, aims and endeavours to zero! You are at your weakest point in this entire process right now. So sharpen those pencils again. Thinking alone is no good, but thinking and writing might get you there.

We are not accustomed to stating categorically what we are going to have, even though as children it was second nature: 'When I'm big, I'm going to have a car, an aeroplane, a big house and a big farm with thousands of golden hamsters.' If we could just harness the power of imagination we had then! As adults, we are more subdued. We don't go around saying we are going to be earning twice as much next year, but simply wait and see.

There is an element of excitement attached to knowing what you want, after honestly opening up to yourself. When you have clear ideas of the type of things you want in your life, there will be an air of *great expectation in you*. That assumes you have disposed of the negative connotations about having goals. If you believe that your gain is another's loss, either you are an austere person by nature, or you don't understand the reason for the gift of life you have in you. Be clear on this point, and look forward to a bright future.

LEVEL IV: THE GOAL ZONE

We discovered earlier that there are two distinct types of goal: material and personal. You prepared inventories of how these stand with you at the present time. Then you gave some thought to possible 'wants' in your life. Those wants were extensions of your present reality and circumstances. You may have scratched your head getting to Level III, but you feel satisfied that your present situation can improve if you just apply yourself a bit. So far, you've relied on *logic and the reasoning mind*, suitably focused on the situation you are in, and possibly tired of. You have used your imagination to come up with several possibilities, rather than more proof to call yourself a failure. The process automatically comes up with 'wants'. You are quite an expert at this, aren't you?

To attempt to reach the goal zone, take a leap across the boundary, and demonstrate that you have learned something about being an Open Person. You can do it! Jump!

The question now is whether or not you will continue into Level IV with only a list of basic wants: 'I want a better job', 'I want more money', 'I want new friends', 'I want to control my behaviour', and so on. You have reached the point of truth: a boundary of personal subtleties tied to *real change*. Are you pursuing *unconditional goals*, or *expanded wants*?

The procedures used in reaching Level III led you to possibilities which might become goals. Whichever of these possibilities you choose to carry into Level IV, the material and personal aspects are interrelated. On crossing the boundary, then, remain flexible and open. If starting a business is the thing for you, then so be it. Think of the personal qualities you'll need for that business. Whatever your ambitions, consider what type of person you will have to be to 'fit' the bill comfortably. Will you need people skills? Confidence? Communication flair? Innovation? Untiring patience?

Let your thoughts run free, but stay focused. Don't let the restraining influence of Level III take the fun out of Level IV. You might say the wants of Level III are attainable, with a little effort and control. They are safe, easily-visualized baby goals, based on what you know best. They are active decisions based on available facts and feelings. Ah, but remember what was said about dreamers, that they were the ones to watch? Well, feel free to dream a bit. Who knows what might come up? Have fun!

PERSONAL GOALS

These come first. The aim isn't to become a bad-mouthed, unforgiving, stressful, immature and opinionated millionaire! If your personal goals are in order, you will find that the material ones will be less difficult to achieve, and to enjoy.

Return to Chapter 5 and consider both the questions and the answers you gave in the Personal Review. In particular, check these:

Personal Attributes
    Self-confidence is a must. Are you in agreement?
    Persistence took you this far. Are you still in?
    People really do matter. Are you having problems there?
    Does change give you nightmares or excitement?
Interpersonal Maturity
    Do you agree that others might know more than you?
    Insecurities are like shadows. Can you name yours?
    Is the external world still getting to you?
    Have you really tried to be an Open Person?
Skills
    You must have some skills, or you're being hard on yourself! Are
    your skills 'you' or have they just happened by default?
    Could present skills lead on to other things, given some
    imagination?
Special Skills
    Do you consider these secondary or important?
    Are you embarrassed by these private skills?
    Could you sell or apply these skills in any way?
Satisfying Returns
    Have you noticed any strong patterns here?
    Is money the only factor in any of these activities?
    Have you felt the sheer pleasure in doing them?
    Were they things that you feel you must continue?

Direction
Are you adding up to anything other than money?
Have you any faith in anything, including yourself?
Are you reading all this without belief?
Has apathy got a firm hold of you?

Personal goals are easy to define, but difficult to implement. Growth is demanding and frustrating. Your goal might be to have a cheerful disposition, but gloomy circumstances ridicule your efforts. So that means you have to persevere, because being cheerful in a gloomy environment is the ultimate test. (It may actually overthrow the gloominess!) We often consciously avoid the goals which we know will give us the most problems and pain, but they are essential to our progress. And if you think that by simply writing goals you will solve problems, think again. You must *want* the goals to happen, and you must *change your behaviour* as far as that demands. So don't have a goal on paper that you set out to circumvent and defy!

YOUR GOALS, YOUR STYLE

Study what you developed in Level II (Feelings) under the headings 'Personal' and 'Relationships'. Are you aware of the weaknesses you have in these areas, and do you have some ideas of what you want to change? Refer to your work in Chapter 5 to gather more clues, and allow yourself a warm-up session to work through these ideas on paper. Once you have the picture reasonably focused, draft up some goals. Since they are yours, and yours alone, write them in your own style and choice of language. This is important, for copying set pieces from another's list has no personal connection with you, even if the nature of the goal is identical.

To give you a structure to work towards, examples of personal goals follow. Notice the sequence of preparing the background before drafting the goal. Although the result is merely a page of words, make sure you think through your motivation in building each goal. Write your goal in the present tense, as though it is already true. And feel the power of your own words. I know it sounds obvious, but think *positively* while you are writing the words. The right frame of mind gives your goals vitality. Positive thinking and attitude do achieve results. For example, telephone sales reps are urged to *smile* as they canvass. The customer picks up the positive, friendly, *winning* style...and buys!

If you are a shy person, and feel that this holds you back in many things, 'confidence' is an obvious choice of goal. Then, as you explore the reasons why you want to be more confident, face up to the very things that cause you embarrassment (awkward speech, hand waving, agitation). *Visualize* what you might look like if you controlled your breathing, sat erect, looked the person in the eye without blushing and so on. That is what is meant by *feeling the power of your own words*. Trust your feeling nature more than your intellect. When your goal rings a certain bell within you, it must be overdue. If a goal feels right, if it raises your interest and excitement, then it's right for you.

List of Personal Goals: Full Form

PATIENCE
Background When a report has to go out at work, I wind up like an alarm clock. I always get my side of things done, even if I work late all week. But it's when it reaches the publication and binding stage that I get impatient, because I have to rely on so many people to get it out. When my back is turned, they're off to have a coffee or have a smoke. Often I tell them to clear out and I do the damned thing myself. I know that if I carry on like this, in the end my health will suffer. Other people are simply going to give me a heart attack. Besides, after these panic episodes, I find I can't get along with the rest of the staff.

Goal I plan the report operation long before the crunch. I study the steps involved and see where the bottle-necks are. I invite all the print-room and word-processing people to a meeting. I'm the chairperson, but they do the talking. We work out a system. Before each report is at the final stages, we have a strategy meeting for an hour, to agree on what we're all doing. I tell myself the time is worth it, and relax in the knowledge that we are a team in control. The result of this: I am a patient person.

SELF-RESPECT
Background I lost my job six months ago. I've tried all the usual ways to get another, but by now I'm sure people will say, 'Well, if that person was any good, they'd have a job by now.' I can see it in their faces if I actually get to an interview. I think my skills are out of date and I'm too fed up to go on any courses, free or not. All the things

you think you'll do if you didn't have to work, well, I don't do them. I've stopped seeing my friends. All I can talk about is not having a job, and all I can do is put myself down. I tend to wear older, shabbier clothes. I doze off in a chair. I watch TV without concentrating at all. I sleep in regularly. I eat when I feel like it. I know I'm on some sort of downward spiral.

Goal Every day, I achieve *something* to get myself up and running again, even if it's a small thing. Each day, I review what I did to improve my self-respect, *however small*. I actually forget I'm unemployed, and tell myself that my daily 'work' is experiencing life as normal, but I don't have to physically *go* to work. I consider myself 'self-employed'. I treat myself as equal to any person with a job; I am not inferior in any way. I actually feel good, having re-established my value as a person.

WILLPOWER

Background I've tried working on a plan for improving my life and career before. It didn't get off the ground. I think that's when my son had measles or something. After a public speaking course I was inspired to be a lecturer at the local college. I filled in the forms, but pulled out before the interview. I did enrol for an Open Learning Course in psychology, but I couldn't see myself getting a diploma. So I stopped doing the assignments and lost my fee.

I really want to do something and my mind's full of ideas, but looking back, all I can see is a sorry trail of pipe-dreams and false starts. What a waste of time and money! If only I could finish a project, perhaps I'd change my butterfly style.

Goal I have found an interest that endures the test of time. From the start, I have stuck to it, even when I must deal with other problems and distractions. I keep a journal, and note down every day what I did to bring my special interest forward. My partner supports me by discussing what my interest is about, asking specific and searching questions to see if I'm progressing! When I see results on this project, I will select another interest and make sure it reaches completion. I welcome this habit of imposed self-discipline.

Are you getting the general idea? Do you see how goals can be developed from the raw data loosely contained in your 'wants'? It is important to work through the reasoning behind each goal you set, otherwise you are being a child: I want, I want, I want. All the goals in these examples are rooted in a practical environment, though your own might have nothing to do with work frustrations or surviving a setback. But the goal process is very flexible, so use it for your specific needs. You can be imaginative and resourceful. Design your own goals around the format given, and bring out the facts and the rationale, using your energetic, but focused mind. Shape your goals in a way that is appropriate to you, but bear the following points in mind.

GOALS ARE POSITIVE AFFIRMATIONS

Notice that no goal dwells on the problems you are trying to overcome: Don't needlessly remind yourself that you are below the mark in a goal. For example, you might be a selfish, inconsiderate oaf. In your goal, don't write: 'I will try to stop being a selfish, inconsiderate oaf.' Rather, write: 'I am a giving, considerate person, full of generosity and respect for others.' And never say 'I'm going to...' Say 'I am...' You are invoking the self-suggestive apparatus here. Tell yourself you are great, and you will be great. Whether it's curing a stammer or having a winning way with kings, the possibilities are endless.

GOALS ARE INTIMATE AND HERALD CHANGE

This book cannot give you a catalogue of personal goals to thumb through, nor the convenience of picking some off-the-shelf. That is making life too easy for you. Besides, your goals are for you alone. You need them, so you develop and define them. Don't overlook the fact that you will be applying them and improving your lot with them!

Generally speaking, you have more chance of achieving your personal goals than ambitious material ones. That is because they are so close to you, and you understand the need more clearly. However, they are perhaps the more tiring, because you are bringing intimate, stressful changes into your life. Most personal goals demand changes in your behaviour, and the way you approach the day's events. Each experience contacts you in a new way when you have set yourself the goal to handle it differently. Allow yourself to change.

MATERIAL GOALS

The scope is open here – you can be as timid or as flamboyant as you wish. I would counsel you to err on the wild side! Too much restraint will make you limit possibilities that really should be within your grasp. Your background or your personal hang-ups have nothing to do with the type of material goals you might want to set. If you have a problem with self-confidence, why should that stop you from owning a harpsichord or a racehorse?

Be reasonable though. Everyone is not going to have a Lear Jet, and a Daimler to meet them as they step ashore from their luxury yacht. But if you honestly believe that is where you want to be, then that is your goal. Why deny it? It is of no consequence whatsoever that you cannot buy these items right now. Who said anything about now?

As you grow into the pattern of commanding success for your life, the possibilities will present themselves to you. And as an Open Person, with a clear idea of where you are going, you will know the moment an opportunity arrives.

So, choose your material goals with ambition appropriate to your real desires. It is foolish to choose a Jaguar XJS with pink seats just because one of your latest lovers got theirs repossessed in their sudden downfall! Similarly, don't expect wealth to solve all your problems. Rich people, more than any other group, have a tendency to commit suicide. That doesn't mean that all rich people are statistically unhappy – it just implies that they can be particularly fragile people when the merry-go-round spins too fast. Money does not remove the basic human insecurities we all suffer from. In fact wealth has a peculiar power to distort reality, introducing excesses and imbalances. Hence the necessary order of personal goals first, material goals second.

In order to fully determine your material goals, you should review your inventory of material things and assets. Know where you stand. You have qualified your Level III 'wants'. But are you restricting your possibilities? Be adventurous! Reach beyond Level III. You may have some ideas bubbling over the boundary already. Stay open and stretch yourself, setting fear and restraint aside. Since the field is so large, it might help to list all the things that catch your eye, then eliminate the absurd and the inappropriate. Pretend that you have won a million on a lottery or a draw. How would you spend it? Go on, draw up a list. Imagine that you have been unconditionally commanded to spend or forfeit the money! In this spirit of make-believe, it seems easier to define material goals, doesn't it? Look at the list below to give you some ideas – you can prune your list down with a little reason and focus.

List of Material Goals: Full Form

HOUSE
Background We live in a very basic house; the walls are so thin we can hear the neighbours sneezing. Most weekends, there's a party somewhere. Every time a door slams, you would think there's someone in our place. The garden is tiny. We can seldom get our car parked near our own door. I have seen the doctor and had a mild sedative for a while. My partner cannot concentrate on anything creative at home, because of the distractions. We have talked to the neighbours, but the results have never been worth the distress following each confrontation. When the adjoining neighbours are all out, we feel like different people, relaxed and less tensed-up. What we would like is to move to somewhere nice.

Goal We own a beautiful house within 40 minutes driving time of the city. It is a three-bedroomed bungalow, set back from the road, and a comfortable distance from the nearest house. It has two bathrooms and a garage/workshop. The neighbours nearby are people like ourselves who love peace around them. They are friendly and helpful to us.

CAR
Background I have a small 1.3 litre 2-door car, now four years old. It's good basic transportation, but starting to give problems. I have driven many other cars, and always prefer a 2.0 litre engine at least. I'm not one of those people that wish to make a 'statement' centred around the car they drive. I just feel that cars are important to me, my only vice and luxury!

Goal I own a Saab 9000 Turbo S, 16 valve, 5-door, with all the options I like to see in a quality car. It is finished in metallic silver with dark grey seats. There is a quadraphonic speaker system, with AM/FM cassette and graphic equalizer. It has all-electric power windows, central locking system and an anti-theft alarm. The windows are tinted the same density as the sunroof. I enjoy the exhilaration of driving it.

MY OWN BUSINESS
Background I fix photocopying machines, and I'm on call seven days a week. I know I'm good at my job, and I've recently finished a home-study course in computer printer maintenance. I've just realized

that I could do the same work and have my own business. I'm certain I could make the same money, possibly a lot more, and I'd be my own boss. My family think it's a great idea. A friend of mine (employed but restless) repairs computers, so we have a super combination. I've never tried a business before, though, and I must admit, the idea makes me very anxious.

Goal I have a business partnership with my friend. Together we have captured at least 50 per cent of the office equipment repair and servicing work in this town. We keep spares and equipment in my garage. I have taken delivery of a van to make the collection operation more efficient. I have a rule that providing the work gets done, both partners can enjoy two days off a week to share with their families.

Heady stuff, isn't it, to just sit down at your desk and specify *exactly* what you want, right down to the number of bathrooms! You do want those things you have specified, don't you? If not, now is the time to pick the essential goals from the nonsense ones. But remember that no goal you want badly enough is ever nonsense.

PORTABLE GOALS

The 'Full Form' goals, both Personal and Material, must now be reduced to a pocket version you can carry about with you. The justification is done. Now you have to *concentrate* on what you have finally set down on paper. To make it more convenient, condense your goals into 'Short Form'. State what you will have, and give some brief explanatory detail if appropriate, but write in the present tense, as if you have already achieved your goals: 'I own a three-bedroomed bungalow, set back from the road...' and so on.

THE REALITY OF SETTING AND ACHIEVING GOALS

Are your goals ridiculous and impossible? Will you succeed? Can you put your hand on your heart, and say with certainty, that you know where the boundary lies between possible and impossible? Are you *determined* to succeed? Have faith in yourself and the wonderful mystery of life!

Some goals will create some concern with your partner or your friends. Firstly, they might think you've gone quite silly. Well, you are an Open Person: why not allow them their opinion of you? Then they'll point out that your goals are totally inconsistent with your present lifestyle and situation. By telling people what you're up to, you invite the big hammers in. They may smash up your resolve to make a better life for yourself and those around you. Will you give them that power? When the time comes to start implementation of your goals, tell only who you must. Meanwhile, keep it all to yourself and supportive collaborators. Remember, you always want to solicit positive feedback from others.

VISUALIZATION: THE MAGIC KEY TO YOUR FUTURE

As you were thinking and writing about your goals, did you feel that curious thrill of detachment: being with your goals? Did you see yourself as a confident, well-groomed, articulate and greatly admired person, doing the things you do best, driving away in your new Mercedes? Or waving to your sister and her husband, as your cruise ship left the quayside? Did you see it? Were you there?

Children daydream best. Sometimes they can invent characters who become better friends than real boys and girls. But adults, too, often have dream-like fantasies. Have you ever had scenes flash before you, when you were bored in a traffic jam, or waiting for someone? And in night-time dreams, have you ever wondered who some of the characters are? Where do these strangers come from, the dream people with real personalities? How can our minds invent fully developed people to inhabit our dreams, with mannerisms, tone of voice and even touch? How do we achieve such fantastic things so easily? Are they real or imaginary?

You took your goals to the short-form stage. Seriously, did you or did you not visualize the goal as being fulfilled, with you at the centre of it? You were driving your vintage Bentley. You were able to smell the cooking from the kitchen of your own restaurant. You could see the form of your lover beside you, just as you dreamed. Well, were you, could you?

Try the 'objects' game. Have someone select 10 ordinary things from around the house, and place the items on the floor or table, covered up with a cloth. Ask the person to remove the cloth for 10 seconds, then replace it. As fast as you can, write down the list of objects.

What methods did you use to recall the objects? Did you rely on memory alone, vision, familiarity, word retention...or yes, visualization? Your eyes have no memory, but the visual stimulus is much greater than others we have. A written list of the objects would be forgotten, even if you devised a mnemonic, but a 10-second visual presentation leaves an indelible impression. The vision is real, for hours, years afterwards.

The same basic process can be used to prepare elaborate visual constructs in our minds. Let's imagine you must make a presentation to a sizeable audience next week; you are nervous. A few quiet minutes spent visualizing yourself on the stage, giving the talk, answering questions *and enjoying* it will put you at ease. It will also help you prepare, to walk the ground as it were. Entertainers, athletes and TV personalities commonly use this simple visualization technique to achieve high performance. Play games with your mind! *Imagine your goals with you in them. Feel* the things you want. Mentally experience the personal changes you want in your life. See them! *Be* them!

MOVING ON

You now have your goals, for better, not worse. They are your goals and you honestly want them to materialize. You have listed them, edited them and polished them for easy reference and recall. Now what?

After this concentrated and intense exercise, it is best to leave goals for a while, and study the process of change. Change must be understood as a powerful tool in your consciousness. It is at the core of goal achievement. Generating goals has been a serious business for you: it has effectively specified your future. The objective now is to learn how you will fulfil these goals.

There is no goal without a purpose, and no purpose without a method. Stay with it; you are doing really well.

REVIEW
1 By carefully researching and constructing goals, you have focused on the direction you wish to take.
2 The Open Person approach has expanded your horizons – to the type of goal, and level of ambition.
3 You have identified closely with goals which you have designed. They have 'personality', which means they are unique to you – ultimately part of you.
4 The practice of creative visualization has brought your goals to life and focused your energy on achieving them.

9 Everything is Change

Without time, change has no meaning. And without change, time would stop.

Alvin Toffler

OVERVIEW

Setting goals can be a fascinating exercise: it gives us a sense of direction. But these dreams are confined to paper unless we change our attitudes, behaviour and focus of energy. Achieving goals is essentially a process of *programmed change*.

Visualizing completed goals allows us to measure the distance between our target and our present position. The shortfall is made up by applied effort and fundamental change. Some goals require time to reach fruition, but the basic rules are the same. Calling up creative change is a *process of mind*. We are bound to change, just as nature is. Our attitude to change, and our willingness to co-operate with it, determines the progress of goals we set.

PAPER DREAMS OR CHANGE?

You now have your goals and the urge to do something with them. That is a significant milestone along the way. However, you may have to brace yourself for an anti-climax. Laziness, fear of the future, even fear of success will start to creep into your thinking. Given some momentum, these feelings may make you disheartened. You can define goals with excitement and all the best intentions in the world, then lose sight of the dream. But there is one absolute you can rely on: change. All your dreams are on paper alone *unless you change*. And change you will, once we have done some more work! We learn very difficult skills over the years, and to the ones we like, we apply effort willingly. Who's to say that learning the skill of arranging a better life is too difficult to try?

CAUTION: NOT EVERYONE WILL LEND SUPPORT

When you want to change your life, you are mostly changing only one person: yourself. It can only be assumed that your goals require changes for the better (why would they be for worse?) So certain people close to you will lend support, especially if they see the muddle you are in at present. Good supporters are precious, and confiding in them sometimes will not harm you, so don't be suspicious or embarrassed.

As you make changes to yourself, however, your wider social circle may also have to change. Your goals may necessarily lead you away from certain people presently in your social or work life. Some of these people will form major hurdles, if they know of your aims and consider them peculiar or threatening. They will criticize, laugh, tease and generally block your progress. (Remember what was said on self-image? Well, take care: it's fragile.) So why tell such people what you are aiming for, if all they will do is laugh at you? There is nothing to be gained by casually revealing or showing off your goals in public (pearls unto swine?) In fact, it dilutes the creative energy you have mustered around you. So every time negative people invade your creative space, *shove them out again!* That's right, push!

CHANGE SHOCK

Change invites 'what if' scenarios. What if I became successful, less self-centred, more confident? How would others feel? Would they accept me? Would I be a stranger, a new creation? Would I lose a piece of myself, a piece I can't get back? Would I have to work harder? Would I face even more pressure?

If your goals are for you, then things *cannot* get worse; they can only get better! Get rid of your fear and procrastination. Your terror of failure is unbecoming to you. Stay resolute: you've come this far, haven't you?

Life isn't a pawn shop. Understand that you are gaining, not losing. If you give advice to someone, do you not still have the knowledge that you started with? When you show kindness, do you then have less to give to the next person? You are not dealing with finite cakes and slices here; it's more like the loaves and fishes. The more you give, the more you have to give. It's abstract, but it's wonderful. Change is not a herald for coming disaster. The popular consensus, the first instinct, is that change is to be feared. Yet you have everything to gain through change, *especially* change you induce for yourself. Look forward to better things, think positively, and *smile!* You are in full control.

THE PROCESS OF CHANGE IS SUBTLE

In anything worthwhile we do or experience, change is necessary to accomplish the levels of satisfaction we desire. Understanding the process is not the difficult stage by any means. *Accepting change and allowing it to happen* are the two areas which challenge us. We must also realize that change is *stressful*. Stress is such a significant topic, in fact, that the next chapter is devoted to it, but our immediate discussion first requires a quick definition to relate change and stress.

The term 'desirable stress' sounds paradoxical. We have been conditioned to believe that stress can only be a harmful agent. But it is quite valid. When we want to induce change in our lives, we must *accept stress* as part of the package. Inviting it into our lives may appear irresponsible and unhealthy. But stress comes in two forms: constructive and destructive. Desirable stress is constructive. Yes, it raises our level of excitement and gets the adrenalin flowing, but we should consider it as desirable. Why? Simply because it gives us that *vital application of pressure and urgency* we need to get going. Put the pressure on and don't worry about taking on too much – you'll grow into it as you go.

So what are we waiting for? Let's get our show on the road! Having optimistic goals is the first prerequisite, and an open mind has given you these goals. An open mind will also help you to achieve them. Before this can happen, though, the *mechanisms of change* must be appreciated.

There are four major steps in the change process:

Appeal to the Open Person Within
Soften your rigid attitudes.
Recognize your current imperfections and shortcomings.
Create a climate of *desirable stress*.

Decide to Welcome Change
Justify your decision to replace old with new.
Accept the *inevitability* of change without resistance.
Show your *confidence* in the procedure.
The Input of the Goals
Visualize each goal as you imagine it completed.
Personally *commit* yourself to your goals with effort and time.
Live your goals, fulfil them.
Results
Practise some self-examination and *assessment*.
Go back and *update* your goals as required.
Identify with the new possibilities and take full control.

Change begins its life as a recognition of wanting something else, or something better. Once we discover that the change process is consistent *and works*, we know it has substance and learn to trust it. Old things look old, new things begin to look new. We only learn to appreciate how change will help us when we accept its inevitability. The process is straightforward. To start things off, we consciously *visualize* our new situations in full detail. Then we mentally focus our goals. Finally, if we honestly apply the level of commitment required, we stimulate the change process to give us completed goals. It is really that simple.

To begin with, however, replacing old ways with new ones is seldom accepted easily. We want the new, but the old must be left intact – just in case the new way is a flop, or is too fast for us. So we keep dragging the old situation about in reserve.

To combat this, the Open Person will find ways to loosen up, to soften rigid ideas, and let new ideas flood in. This causes a rise in stress level, but that is good in its own way. It draws attention to the process and generates excitement in our consciousness. Change is like parachute jumping: it focuses the mind, gets the adrenalin pumping, and promises thrills for those who dare.

FOCUS ON GOALS, ON CHANGE

Your goals must be placed at the centre of the change process. This allows personal control over change, which is the very thing you want. Whatever your goals, see yourself *attached to them*. Visualization is a beautiful gift. Enjoy it, and learn to use it as a tool in the real world, to bring images and dreams to realization.

As you begin to see the first changes manifesting themselves in your life you will feel more confident and satisfied with your efforts, further reinforcing the change process as a worthwhile and exciting development. Material goals can be highly visible in the mind's eye: 'That's my Porsche.' Personal goals are somewhat subjective: 'I think I'm friendlier.' Be aware of little steps. You may wish to reconsider the priorities or specific content of your goals; that is your prerogative. If the Porsche hasn't come yet, that doesn't mean everything has gone wrong. Relax and wait. Take the necessary steps – it won't come in the next post by wishing alone.

TIME IS A KEY FACTOR

Each person has a specific rate of assimilation to change. Don't try to have satisfied goals in a matter of weeks, or demand great leaps forward on all your goals at once. You have to learn to wait for things, and be willing to apply unfailing effort while waiting. It might take a whole year or more to adapt to a significant change like the death of a family member, a divorce or a change in location. Don't worry. Similarly, you cannot expect to suddenly change from a miserable, self-centred, opinionated and penniless drifter to a cheerful, generous, open-minded and rich achiever! Be fair to yourself. Find your natural pace and work with it. Why should changing your life be on the express line?

THE PROCESS OF CHANGE IS A PROCESS OF MIND

At this point in the proceedings, you have some insight into the preparation of goals and the nature of change. You probably feel confident that you can accomplish your goals through effort and conscious change. Given time, you will move into that wonderful state of being where things are really beginning to happen. You will notice a pattern unfolding. Small things, or even unrelated events, will show you that yes, there is change here!

The calling up of change is a *process* of mind. Remain open at all times, or you'll block forces you have summoned up.

Jane was blasting leaves off her path with a garden hose, controlling the flow with the nozzle. It occurred to her that if she really wanted to change herself, or at least her way of thinking, the thing to do would be to stick the hose in her ear and flush out all the rubbish in her mind! If only it could be so easy!

Meanwhile she had control over the energy in the water, and the direction of the leaves. The clean path was like a new mind. Then she blasted loose gravel over the path, instead of leaves. That was interesting – she could choose what she put in her mind! But she realized the leaves and the gravel were like thoughts; they were not in control of the hose.

FALSE PROPHETS

Unfortunately, it is hard sometimes to positively establish if change is happening. There is a state we can fall into which looks very like change; it mimics the process so well, we really start believing that transformation has arrived. How can you judge when you are really in the process of change or when you are simply indulging in wishful thinking? (I'm certain I'm less bad-tempered, don't argue with me!)

Quite often the uncertainty begins with some soul-searching which leaves one feeling rather low and in need of a 'quick fix'. This might appear to do the trick, but if it is not based on a firm foundation, it fades.

For example, you may sit down and write out your current situation, as part of a goal-setting exercise, then in a state of anxiety, restlessness and unhappiness, you lash out in all directions: 'I'm talented! I'll show them! I have brains! I have class! I know what I want!' If we can recognize this volatile state for what it is, then we can transform all the restless energy (desirable stress) into constructive goals, geared to what we want to change. But without shape and form, the steps of change are broken, loose, slippery. You will scramble about just trying to keep your balance.

The early stages of change will always include a state of anxiety. How else will you move yourself out of apathy? But anxiety is healthy, if you know how to channel its energies into action. Seizing the creative energy generated by your anxiety is good. It pushes you into new areas of self-awareness, without jeopardizing your health or mental well-being. 'I feel the pressure, but I really do have some control over things!' But beware! The hazards of undisciplined zeal may catch you just at this point. When you are exhilarated by the vague promise of better things, by the quick fix to your problems, you can fall for the wayward cousin of change: Big Mouth.

Big Mouth likes to tell everyone what he or she is going to do: going to have the house in the exclusive development, the flash car, the great career, the exotic holidays, going to eat in expensive restaurants and retire at 40. Look out for Big Mouth's brilliant future... Energy soars around such people, making others feel vaguely jealous. But listen. Is there any substance there? Any compassion, any interest in other people? Are there qualities of honesty, sincerity, generosity, consideration for others less fortunate? Does Big Mouth take time or silence to notice what is really happening, that the whole show is self-centred aggrandizement? Is the successful image of Big Mouth true success? I'm sure you will have your doubts by now.

Energy in this form provides days, weeks perhaps, of wishful excitement and renewed purpose. Then it dissipates, reappearing in spasmodic bursts, but waning to a state very close to depression. How can this be? *You need more than that.* And I will make sure you won't fall into the Big Mouth trap!

CHANGE: THE REALITY OF LIFE

Change is inseparable from nature itself. Few people consciously acknowledge the significance of this. Are you aware of the changing seasons, the subtle changes of trees, hillsides, beaches, plants and grass, rain or shine? Do you grumble when it's stormy, or do you watch the storm, even stand out in it, walk in it? There is nothing so humbling as a long walk in a torrential downpour without coat or sensible shoes! Surrendering to the elements should not be interpreted as a crushing of the human spirit. In fact it can be delicious, a feeling of being truly alive and at one with the world, rather than in opposition to it. Try to see change in the same way: uncomfortable at first, then a little humbling, and finally fantastic and not to be missed!

Take heart from the fact that change is part of our lives. Every organ of our bodies is involved in change. The very humble cell is constantly changing, reforming, dying. Admit it, *you are a creature of change. It is our physiology and our personal reality, every day of our lives.* Rather than forever running from it, become a willing partner with change. Spend a whole day, a week if you like, watching and noting evidence of change. You know you can't get away from it.

The Open Person watches the natural processes of change, tries to experience a *personal closeness* to change, and develops a deep respect for it as a *healing* force. Three things are inseparable: change, time, life.

We should aim for a balance, an understanding of changing what we can, but knowing when to accept things we cannot or should not change. Accepting what is doesn't mean accepting second best, though. When your flight is delayed, for example, you can indulge in

a four-hour tantrum, or buy a book like this and make the best of the
'lost' time. Then that time would be highly beneficial, not lost at all!

What really matters is your attitude to change, and the free-will
choices you make which actually guide change itself. Change can be
used to replace attitudes or poor choices, if you allow it.

CHANGE: PERSONALITY AND POWER

Change is a quiet, purposeful thing. It is more subtle than brassy.
More determined than energetic. More personal than communal. There
are many counterfeit versions of change. So many people are bluster-
ing about, full of anxiety and noise, eager to change the world. But it
is well known that changing the world must begin with changing yourself. And that change process must be discrete, a private thing.

When you decide to effect change in your own life, please respect
the process and respect yourself. Listen rather than speak. Stay open
rather than assuming you have all the answers. Be mindful that you
are essentially creating the future by co-operating with the change process. It's quite awesome, but fascinating.

Change is a powerful force within us, which cannot abide cheap
copies brought in from the external world. The voices of change are
quiet, subtle and always there if you only listen. Stop shouting and
you will hear them. When they do whisper to you, heed them, or you
must set off backwards along the old path. Play games with change
and you will tumble. Make it very clear what you want, declare it, then
accept the reality of personal change.

ATTITUDES ARE CENTRAL TO MEANINGFUL CHANGE

We live in a state of useless worry much of the time. Good attitudes
can help you to avoid uncreative stress, and organize your life more
harmoniously. Some common worry examples, and their 'attitude-
opposites' make interesting study:

SITUATION	RESPONSE
I have a job.	I worry about losing my job.
I'm unemployed.	I worry about not having a job.
I have a job.	I'm thankful for having a job.

I'm unemployed.	I make the very best use of my time.
I have a wonderful partner.	I worry that he/she will leave me.
I have no partner.	I worry that I'll never find anyone.
I have a wonderful partner.	I enjoy our relationship daily.
I have no partner.	I enjoy life, even if I am alone.
I'm healthy.	I worry about being ill.
I'm unhealthy.	I worry about the next complication.
I'm healthy.	I show compassion and help the ill.
I'm unhealthy.	I cope with my problem cheerfully.

SELECTIVE CHANGE WILL PUT YOU WHERE YOU WANT TO BE

The two attitudes say it all. Conscious change helps us to shift from one attitude to the other – hopefully, from one of unhealthy resentment and dissatisfaction to one of accepting what is. That fundamental effort is central to your growth and extends to the business of achieving your goals. Changing your attitudes is difficult. The majority of people grow old with attitudes they should have changed in their youth. That is how difficult it is. Only a few people take up the challenge and accept the hard work required. Are you willing to join them and live a magnificent life?

YOUR WORLD AND YOU

Are you by any chance a pessimist by nature or beaten into passive submission by the problems and despair of the world? Of *course* we are affected by the world. We can't write individual goals to solve global problems, but by making sense of your own situation and problems, is it not possible that the world could be a marginally better place? You might never have any direct influence on stopping wars and disasters. But you could help the people *around you* to lose some of their unproductive despair for a sorry world. The place to begin is within your own consciousness.

All you need to look for now is the *optimistic voice within you*, and begin to listen to it. Stop asking questions all the time. Why does a tragedy like Ethiopia happen in a world of surpluses and food piled in warehouses? Why do people go insane and shoot other citizens? Why do vandals drag our environment down by destroying things? Questions are easy, whether they are raised for world issues, or for personal crises. Senior executives often get there because they have the skill of 'asking the right questions'. But what of the answers? *There is your challenge!*

ROLE MODELS?

You might think of changing yourself into the 'type' of person you would like to be. Perhaps you like Clint Eastwood, Madonna or Bob Geldof. These people are fantastic *as* Clint Eastwood, Madonna and Bob Geldof respectively. But do you think *they* don't have problems? If you mimic the image of another, you may have no more than an idealistic view of yourself: *you don't really exist as you.* (Remember Chapter 3 and being 100 per cent yourself?) Using change to build an imported self-image is dangerous, as well as a complete waste of energy. You must accept yourself as you are, and build on that. Bio-engineers might manage to clone your body before very long, but the idea of changing 'you' into someone else is wild. *Be unique and celebrate that fact.* Better to be a magnificent you than a poor reproduction of someone else!

CHANGE TO GREENER GRASS?

Changing location is sometimes a promising catalyst for change, though it is by no means ideal for everyone. Moving gives you a useful shift in environment: you gain the necessary freedom to work on yourself; your old friends are off the stage; you can act a different role, playing yourself. There is considerable leverage in it. If you think it suits your goal-plan, then consider it.

Many people even emigrate to other countries. Generally the nature of emigration allows the operation of a pioneering spirit impossible in a 'home' environment. Each day is given over to greater progress of self. This attitude adjustment of pioneering into the future is fascinating. Quite mundane, barely ambitious people stretch themselves in ways they would formerly have resisted or criticized. They become more successful both in terms of possessions and personal outreach. It could be argued that the 'good life' of the new country makes it easy, so they couldn't fail. However, *permanent growth does occur in the individual*. The feeling of a better lifestyle may give more confidence, which in turn makes it easier to attract wealth through increased ambition. Environment and freshness are potent catalysts. Don't overlook this possibility.

Remember, though, that location alone cannot alter the stuff of goals and provide the better life you seek; it just gives you a cleaner slate to work with. Your outward behaviour might become more generous, but the inner person may still require attention. You are the same person whether you settle in Toronto or Tobago, Tooting or Toowoomba.

Moving to the good life can be a pipe-dream in itself, unless it is part of the right map and set of goals for your life. For the good life comes from *within*. It is conceived within you and directed by you. Moving might help the process; it will not by itself give you what you really want. If one of your goals is to move to another country in the hope of a 'better life', consider what you are taking with you. Should you leave *yourself* behind, you are simply rushing to be moulded into someone else's property, with a different culture deciding who you are.

TALK WORDS, LIVE THEM

Speak as if you are a failure and you will become the best failure that ever was! 'Oh, I've never had much luck. The system's always against me. Other people get all the chances, the opportunities. I'm stuck in a rut that I can't get out of...' By thinking poor, dejected and defeatist thoughts, you *attract* the very things (and people) you want to avoid. You can add to your misery by constantly discussing the terrible state of the world – not to mention the mess they're making with the new road 'improvements', declining morals, unemployment, violence, the madness of the arms race and the price of onions! Negative words accompany negative themes accompany negative people. *Make that forward passage from negative words to positive words, and the attitudes will change accordingly!* Change your words! Substitute bright thoughts and words in your daily life! Keep the dark colours for funerals!

Jeremy was on his way to a meeting in the city. He crossed the bridge from the railway station and came down the stairs to the busy street. There were canvas fire hoses lying about, some connected to hydrants. This was hose-down day for the tramps who slept rough under the bridge. Water and disinfectant were applied at regular intervals to keep the area sanitary. It was a scene of misery. People struggled to get past on their way to appointments, in a different world. The despair could be felt by anyone who cared to look, but few did.

Then Jeremy noticed a man in his late forties sitting on a reasonably good mattress. He was eating cold baked beans from a can. The unconcerned, peaceful expression on his face made Jeremy smile. The man's situation was clear to all, but there was no despair in his eyes when he smiled in return. The two men both engaged in a silent appraisal of his predicament, but the man eating beans was less disturbed by it than Jeremy was.

Jeremy shifted his gaze to the flamboyant, neatly-arranged poster pinned to the large cardboard box which was this fellow's February shelter. It read: 'This is the home of Marathon Willie, three times a champion and fit as a fiddle. Welcome to my world.'

What we choose to entertain in our minds can have a more profound effect on our outlook and progress than circumstances. For example, suicide is not popular with the folks under the bridges of our world – ending life by self-reason is more common among the middle classes, the educated and the successful. Is that not even more tragic than the despair under our bridges? So choose your thoughts and words with care: your life depends on it.

You have the choice to view this world any way you want. Perhaps your world view is immature at this point in your life. Well, let change help you to get things in perspective. You can start by discarding grey words of despair and negative thoughts which limit both yourself and the world about you.

Surveys among children have shown that a large number see a world without hope. Kids have decided, at a very early age, that the bomb will get us, some incurable disease will drag us off, or everyday violence will do it. Short of annihilation, simply getting a job on leaving school makes the future bleak enough, and children look forward with little hope. They watch violent videos and absorb grey news. They talk to peers and adults with cynical and critical world views. Their behaviour can even degenerate to a state of quasi-autism. (Autistic children see the world as meaningless and confusing; they are frustrated and discouraged by it.) Seldom do they see the good things that are happening. Good things are so rare, they don't know how to deal with them! Good news is 'soft' or 'boring'. How will optimistic goals for the future appeal to them?

This gloomy outlook is not restricted to children. Adults share it, often with more conviction. So make your passage from negative to positive – right now! I think the point has been made; I know you will shake off those negative, limiting thoughts and words.

SUBSTITUTE 'POSSIBLE' – AND GO FOR CHANGE

My recurring theme in this book is to eliminate the concept of 'the impossible'. Get your big broom out and sweep away your broody, defeatist self! Who said you can't do better with your life, that you'll never get out of that rut: was it you? Life is never hopeless.

Start to change by throwing out resentment of your present situation. Be grateful for all you have. It might not be exactly what you want, but don't brood along through life; it does no good for you or your goals. If you are a naturally jealous person, always wishing for the other person's things and qualities, stop it! *You are going to get your own, aren't you?* So concentrate on that, instead of wasting precious energy.

When we decide to change, it must be a daily reality. It cannot be exclusively for work, or kept only for home life. It goes right through your consciousness in all you do. Consciousness is all you have to work with most of the time. *You are limitless, so get out there and experience limitless growth.*

Positive change is a process of faith, when you examine its roots. You don't have to be religious in any way (but note that we all have a religion, even if it's only belief in ourselves). Faith is a great and versatile reality. Its significance cannot be depreciated.

If you are willing to change, you are willing to live. Why deny life to yourself? You have your chances like everyone else. The abilities you have *are* in demand, once you learn to focus them. People *do* want you to be their friend. You *can* succeed at what you have chosen to do. The higher your hopes, the better. *Lift your consciousness up* to take it all in. Find security in yourself first, then work at the business in hand. Trust in change and wait for the results.

REVIEW

1 You have come to terms with the reality of change and can benefit from it, without fear or distress.

2 The development of the Open Person in you has 'softened' rigid attitudes and created 'desirable stress' to motivate you to action.

3 As change occurs (under your control) you have been able to see an encouraging pattern developing – changes for the better!

4 Your entire approach to life has embraced the positive aspects of change, thus 'permitting' goals to be realized.

10   Stress or Distress?

Nothing to do is not to rest; a vacant mind and a slothful body suffer
the distress of deprivation.

Hans Selye

OVERVIEW

Changing our lives is a stressful business. It is important to
understand the nature of stress, and determine how we can work
with it. If we ignore the negative effects of stress, the future
might not be so wonderful: stress could drag us down.

There are well documented 'life stressors' such as death in the
family or divorce. Our phases of life also produce their own
stressful episodes. We must appreciate that stress is a function of
living; only our reaction to it can be controlled.

The concepts of stress and distress are introduced. The former is
natural (even 'desirable') but the latter is ultimately destructive.
We need a pinch of stress to tackle life's challenges and make
progress. But we must also be able to identify distress and successfully contain it.

STRESS

So far we have examined our personal world views and attitudes, and
the concept of being an Open Person. You have defined your wants
and goals. The nature of change has been explored in order to dis-
lodge apathy and insecurity. Here and there I have mentioned stress,
without much definition or elaboration. Now it is time to elaborate,

because goal-setting and goal achievement is a stressful business! The last thing you want now is an overload of stress and no means of coping with it. Understanding stress is your next step towards those goals.

WHERE DOES STRESS ORIGINATE?

Change causes stress. There is no simpler way of putting it. If we had no stress in our lives, then we would be, quite probably, dead. Everything on our life path can be seen as a change, a stimulus, a concern. The great unknown of our individual and collective futures can cause stress, because it is unclear, uncertain and threatening. New technology confronts us at a rate which can often be overwhelming. The throwaway society seems to extend even to people and social change can be too complex to even understand. Some changes are for the good, but others seem unreasonable and confounding. Customs, habits and familiar methods are constantly superseded by new ways and styles. It appears so difficult to adapt, to make sound decisions that are credible.

Changes, situations, circumstances, the stuff of everyday life – they all put us under stress, even though, generally speaking, we tend to associate stress solely with *unpleasant* things in our lives. In fact there are known, quantifiable sources of stress (stressors) which seldom fail to give us trouble. In decreasing order of damage, typical 'life stressors' are:

High Stress
Death of close family member.
Prison sentence.
Financial ruin or serious difficulties.
Infidelity of partner; divorce.
Redundancy, dismissal, unemployment.
Medium Stress
Serious illness requiring medical help.
Failure at college.
Family disputes, problem children.
Work disputes, animosity.
Low Stress
Emigration or foreign posting.
Retirement.
Children leaving home.
Pregnancy.
Mortgage, loan and credit management.

The list focuses on relatively grim events in our lives, events that are difficult to avoid. At any time, we can predict trouble in terms of the stress loading of an individual. Someone faced with perhaps three or four key stressors, with one or two from the top group, may experience physical or mental illness as a direct result. A recently unemployed single parent, for example, highly mortgaged and experiencing teenager rebellion, would be a highly stressed individual. Of course, the degree of damage stress can cause depends on other factors, such as support from family and friends, personal attitude and financial reserves. It should be noted, too, that individuals may cope successfully with stressors high on the list, but go to pieces with something less dramatic, like children leaving home, or relatively simple car troubles. The list is therefore subject to individual response and consideration of personal attitudes and degree of preparation is essential.

WHY YOU NEED SOME STRESS COUNSELLING

Since the effects of stress can be quite undesirable, in fact potentially life-threatening, we must give the topic more than a passing acknowledgement in our progress towards achieving goals. Goal-setting and personal change are not in the above 'life stressor' list, but depending on your specific plans, you may place them in the group of your choice. Becoming an Open Person, developing self-awareness, defining what you want, setting and pursuing goals...these things are positively stressful! Setting out to overhaul one's life is undoubtedly more stressful than Christmas shopping. It might be as stressful as redundancy or a death in the family. Becoming a 'new' person implies a loss of the 'old', for instance, and loss can be seen as a grieving process, which is certainly stressful. This is why we must understand stress and gauge its impact on any programme of self-improvement.

Why bring stress into your life through soul-searching and setting goals anyway? Is that the price to be paid for your change of career, private plane or your custom-designed lifestyle? It does sound depressing talking about stress at the very point where you are impatient to get your goals under way. But I don't want to gloss over such an important issue. There is no escape: *you are going to encounter stress as you work towards your goals* and we have to prepare accordingly. With each change you make, each sacrifice, each application of effort, you are inviting stress into your life, lots of it. But stress need not harm you. In fact, used with understanding, *it may do you nothing but good*. So read this chapter in a positive frame of mind; please don't look on stress as just another grey word!

WHAT EXACTLY IS STRESS?

To begin with, stress is not just nervous tension. It is not a state of panic where everything seems to be going wrong. Quite simply, *stress is the body's natural response to any demand or change made upon it*, a biological cause-and-effect mechanism. Whether you lose a job or find one, you experience stress. When a tile falls from a roof, your body responds to protect you almost instantaneously. If you achieve success in your career or sport, your entire system (body and mind) adjusts to the change, excitement and rewards. Your system even anticipates future demands and prepares accordingly. You don't have to be a surgeon, submarine commander or an air traffic controller to experience high levels of stress – we all get our chance, even in mundane surroundings. Lengthy and absolute definitions are merely academic. *Whether we* suffer *from stress or not is the real issue*. Ominous and distasteful as it sounds, stress is actually quite impartial, neutral. *We* decide if it's good or bad.

I freely admit to having tormented our family cat when I was perhaps seven or eight. Without a doubt, the best game to play with it was 'fur torture'. This involved touching the cat at random intervals at different places on its coat (the simplest of tactile contact), with the approaching hand outside its field of vision.

A few minutes of this and the poor cat would be in a state of extreme displeasure. It would spin around, screeching, paw clawing at its back, angry, confused, excited, ferocious, distressed and irrational. The game could go on like this for perhaps five or six minutes. But then a surprising thing would happen. The cat would grow passive, put up less and less resistance, then become quite depressed and subdued. The game was over (till the next time).

Today, I see the wickedness of my boyhood indifference, but I also see the lessons the cat taught me. Firstly, that some stress can be stimulating, even fun for a while – I'm certain the cat enjoyed the initial teasing and played along for amusement. But secondly, that too much stress brings even the most playful creature to a state of apathy, listlessness and withdrawal.

Abraham Maslow gave us the useful concept of five upwardly-mobile motivation needs. Each step in our life evolution takes us towards what he proposed as 'self-actualization'. Beginning with basic physiological needs (survival essentials like food and shelter), we then attend to the first order psychological need of security (a safe environment). Most of us generally achieve this minimum level. Then comes belongingness, needing to love and be loved, to feel accepted by family, friends and work associates. Recognition and esteem are next in the upward plan: we like attention, praise, status and, if we can earn it, acknowledgement of our uniqueness.

Maslow's ultimate goal of life is the *desire for self-actualization*. This final and very encompassing step marks the truly mature person. The self-actualized individual has a high self-regard, has no need of self-defensiveness, and moves through life with confidence and enthusiasm. He or she could certainly be described as an Open Person, at the peak of the personal success curve. Maslow's theory supposes that we can only progress upwards through the steps once we satisfy the step we are on. Other theorists like C.P. Alderfer remove this slightly restrictive condition, allowing us to develop upwards without waiting. Each step up is not automatic, some pre-ordained human right. Each has to be worked for and that involves stress. *Stress is the essential catalyst for progress*, the vital push that drives us on.

WHAT MAKES YOU GET UP IN THE MORNING?

Do you launch into each day just because the alarm clock goes off, or is there some other, more meaningful purpose? You must have wondered why you make the effort, beyond the obvious reasons such as earning a living or getting children off to school. You might call it life-force, mission, latent energy, the projection of self or soul. Perhaps it is the feeling of being useful to oneself and others, of making some contribution to the scheme of things.

This notion of purpose comes into play when someone encounters retirement without any preparation. We often witness a collapse in terms of depleted self-esteem, uselessness, reduced energy level and general demotivation. Retirement may signal well-earned leisure and renewal, but too often it produces debilitation, illness and depression. Men in particular are prone to post-retirement stress and even premature death. They seem to have less interest in replacing a career with other constructive activities. Women, on the other hand, are usually able to build a support/activity network over the years which cushions retirement from a career. However, women do endure a stressful time when their role of mother is no longer significant and their children leave the nest. This is due to the same desire to be useful.

Feeling useful is, in fact, a vital factor in the life process. It gives us self-worth, if nothing else. If we feel worthless, how can we justify getting out of bed and facing the day? The things we do and the goals we set are part of the process. Setting goals which are clearly out of reach for us, or too modest (just wanting to get by and avoid bother, for example), will both result in unhealthy stress. The executive on a burn-out trajectory grapples with stress, but so does the disillusioned person taking each day as it comes and hating every boring minute of it. The example of the cat is appropriate: *a little stress is stimulating and may even be fun; too much for too long can be unhealthy distress.*

STRESSED-OUT OR SIMPLY MOTIVATED?

Although we often blame circumstances for every misfortune (or stress) in our lives, many of our troubles are due to our own attitudes and approach to life. An example: consider a busy, efficient and cheerful waitress coping with busy tables, constant demands and low tips. Her colleague might be moody, bad-tempered, abrasive, harassed and incompetent. One waitress is helpful, the other rude. One enjoys the work despite the stresses, the other finds fault in everything and would like to throw plates of soup at the customers. The workload and setting might be identical for both, the relevant (observable) stresses the same. The key to the behaviour of the waitresses is *motivation*, not stress.

LIFE EVENTS AND STRESS PHASES

We cannot stop at motivation, however. Although motivation often appears at the scene of stress (and influences our method of dealing with it), there are other issues to consider. It is too easy to say that attitude shapes our world view, declare that setting a few realistic goals is good for a person, and then leave everything dangling there. Have we not heard of identity crises, mid-life crises and other uncomfortable reactions to life? These episodes are natural, not symptoms of mental illness or bad luck of some sort. You may not be having a full-blown crisis at the moment, but then in progressing this far you have had to take a long hard look at your life-map. Have you noticed any discomfort, perhaps a little stress?

We all progress through the various phases of life: childhood, youth, young adulthood, relationships, career, self-analysis, maturity. Think about the phases of life. We are all caught up in them. Understanding your life phases may help you see things more clearly. Maybe you'll review your goals in this new light.

RESPONDING TO STRESS

The important point to grasp is that *stress can be a positive or negative experience.* You respond to stress in much the same manner as you respond to setting goals and achieving them – with enthusiasm and action, or with disgust, lethargy and foreboding. Virtually every cell in your body will react to *any* stimulus that comes along. We fight or take flight, adapt, endure or collapse.

Sometimes it is better to run than to fight, or to tolerate something rather than try to change it. Life is a continuous process of stimulation – choice – reaction. If things are going wrong, you might boldly choose to take on the whole world (resistance), or simply bow before the inevitable (endurance). A person might slight you. Do you seek revenge or quietly rise above pointless hostility and move on? Similarly, sudden loss of employment can be seen as the end of your world, or perhaps the essential shock (desirable stress) you need to discover a new career, a new and more exciting life. Studying for and taking exams might also be filled with tension, anxiety and stress, but passing them opens up new, exciting horizons.

Living without a sprinkle of stress would be bland; nothing truly interesting or exciting would happen. A total lack of stimulation and corresponding stress would make us feel so uncomfortable we would feel compelled to change our situation! But the stimulation, event, change or development will always come. Be sure of that! How will you choose? How will you react? Resist – for how long? Adapt – with what consequences or opportunities? Take flight – to where?

PERSONALITY FACTORS: TYPE A AND TYPE B

Studies on heart attack victims have given us the now household terms 'Type A' and 'Type B' people. Type A is achievement-directed, time obsessed, aggressive, self-demanding, impatient, workaholic and indifferent to relaxation. Type B takes pleasure in simple things, balances work demands, is less ambitious, laughs more and does everything at a relaxed pace. Which type are you?

We have to be careful about classifying people. Let's examine this properly, to be sure we form the right conclusions. Type A people (the high achievers) might be burning the candle at both ends, fighting off the alligators to beat deadlines and achieve more and more. They would invite more heart attacks, wouldn't they? But Type B people (the casuals) might be so laid back they develop stress ulcers anyway from frustration at never achieving anything! We are led to believe that Type As get more out of life: all their goals come true. Type Bs are then seen as non-achievers, rather dull people you would never ask to a party. This book *does not* promote Type A behaviour.

Rather, it promotes a *balance*. In fact, Type B, *properly understood*, is the more likely model for success. A *balanced* Type B can be just as successful as any high-flying Type A, but without all the unhealthy stress. Or, if you prefer the other approach, a *balanced* Type A would also fit the bill.

DISTRESS

Certainly we do have a limit for adaptation and tolerance of stress and stressful situations. If a job is unsatisfactory, for example, we cope for a time, then experience signs of burn-out. How much stress is enough? Too much, and the situation deteriorates. The same cycle occurs in unsuccessful human relationships: there is a finite limit to our store of coping and adaptability. This is when stress is damaging and the best name for it is *distress*. One version is healthy, the other quite destructive. It might be nice (though stressful) to embrace your partner, but positively *distressing* to witness that same partner cavorting with a stranger.

As we grow older, cumulative distress leaves its mark. Our store of adaptation and resistance runs out and irreparable damage is done. Distress can damage health, or at least lower resistance to disease. Ageing itself is linked to distress, a gradual wearing-down of the human organism, just like a machine.

STRESS ANALOGIES

It is useful to consider the analogy of stress as used in engineering. In simple terms, a structural member subjected to load will encounter stress. This is defined as the total load divided by the cross-sectional area of the member. Normally, an allowable stress level is specified, related to operating conditions, risk, temperature of service and consequences of failure. This establishes the safety factor, which prevents the structure ever reaching a stress level which invites failure. In any structure, if loading increases to the ultimate stress level, the structure breaks. One mode of failure is *fatigue*, where repeated cycles of loading may cause the structure to fail long before its ultimate strength. The stresses caused by these cycles can be well below the allowable stress, and fatigue has been a perplexing problem for designers. There are ground rules and theories to follow, but accurate prediction of failure is impossible. Some materials defy the theories and go on bearing loads; others fracture and self-destruct long before their predicted 'fatigue life' elapses.

When engineers talk of stress, they often use terms like 'stress and the behaviour of bodies', 'endurance limit', 'yield point' and 'fatigue stress history'. Medical people talking of stress use terms like 'General Adaptation Syndrome' (response, resistance, exhaustion), 'biological stress resistance' and so on. We humans can be understood both as machines and as bio-molecules! Both sciences are relevant in our study of stress. However, the engineer's task may be easier than the psychologist's. Quite honestly, there are more definitive and numerate ways of describing stresses in a bridge truss than in a person. Would you fly in an aircraft where the stresses were critically high, the fatigue life was exceeded and the plane had a history of heavy landings? In the same sense, would you take on excessive responsibilities while undergoing a few of life's unpleasant stressors and showing signs of falling in a heap? The analogy is apt, but of course we are more conservative with machines than with our bodies and minds.

BAD NEWS, GOOD NEWS

Admit it. You are going to experience stress all your life. Activities which are stressful (but *rewarding*) make life dynamic, stimulating, meaningful. Driving, skiing, cycling down long hills, career development, artistic endeavour, relationships, travel, higher education: they place demands – sometimes enormous demands – on your system, but aren't they worth it? When a large presentation or a critical meeting goes well, doesn't it feel *good* afterwards? When you build that boat and it sails like a dream, isn't it just *great*? When you get that diploma or degree in your hand after years of struggle, don't you feel *proud*? Working up to the event might have been hard work and certainly stressful. But somehow people can remain motivated and achieve their goals, stress or not. We can call this elusive spirit 'satisfaction', 'thrill', 'reward', 'participation', 'achievement', whatever. It remains that active, motivated participation is the best antidote for stress we'll ever find. Successful people usually experience much *more* stress than the average person. But they channel it through their activities in a creative way and learn to enjoy life even more. Their level of enthusiasm and involvement can be intense: half-hearted attitudes are driven out. They simply do not allow unproductive stress (distress) to take control. This does not mean suppression of 'bad' experiences leading to neurosis. Rather, it suggests a need for *balance*, self-stability and big-picture perspective – and faith perhaps? Such people's positive attitude tends to feed success, which in turn promotes an uncanny love of life and yet more success. It's as if they have found a mission in life. We can all find this if only we look.

STRESS STIMULATES, DISTRESS DEBILITATES

The list of unpleasant stressors (divorce, redundancy, work pressures, etc.) is more difficult to resolve. Distress is no fun at all and we must understand its dangers if we are to live productive, healthy lives. Too much distress gnaws away at our biological and psychological fabric, progressively lowers our resistance and ultimately kills us. Even if your particular and current stressors are not on the list, your response to unpleasant episodes in your life may make or break you. Heart problems, cancer, digestive disorders, arthritis, insomnia, diabetes, allergies and tooth decay are just some of the physiological problems we invite by allowing distress to take over our lives.

Myalgic Encephalomyelitis (ME), the post-viral syndrome, for example, is a disturbing modern health problem. Research has identified environmental pollutants, diet, lifestyle and food additives as typical factors in its development. In ME cases, the immune system (our inbuilt resistance to disease) becomes overwhelmed by given viruses. And the immune system is thought to be influenced by stress (distress). There is a strong connection here between the organism's ability to resist stress, and disease. Psychosomatic illness is now a highly discussed area of modern medicine. Perhaps clinical illness is virtually all psychosomatic?

Our minds take a beating too: regression, depression, irritability, diminished concentration, nightmares... Many of these things are due to the negative effects of stress.

So it is a fact that unpleasant stressors are likely to be part of your life. Don't let that fact undermine you and cast you into despair. If you understand the process, you are more likely to survive. Just as hospitalized patients may 'lose the will to live', distress may overwhelm your coping reserves. Past failures and setbacks may have taken the spark right out of you; perhaps your health has suffered because of them. Comebacks may seem impossible. There may have been lengthy episodes of personal dissatisfaction, distressing events from the 'bad' list and a complete surrender of the will to apathy and withdrawal. Somehow *you have to confront yourself and do something about it.* Isn't that really what this book is all about, whatever your situation? My axiom is crude but penetrating: *If you have life, why not live the damned thing?*

DECISION TIME: STRESS OR DISTRESS?

All right. You are vaguely aware of being under stress. The first question is: is it stress or distress? Is your situation unpleasant, demanding, tiring, frustrating, confusing and irritating? Are your hackles up over people? Are you facing any topics from the 'life stressor' list? Do you have money problems? Is your job draining you? Do you have no time for relaxation, holidays, exercise? Do you suffer from emotional outbursts, restlessness, depression, muscle tension, headaches, palpitations, insomnia, nervousness? You should be able to identify distress from 'healthy' stress by now. Well, how distressed are you, after considering the above questions?

No matter how bad it looks, you can take action to smooth out your stress and bring yourself back to an even keel. If you have symptoms, then you have problems. But problems do have solutions, fortunately. *Welcome* a healthy pinch of stress, then take *action*, however simple. Action seems to put things into perspective and makes you feel the problem is smaller because it is being confronted. Perhaps you can't see the point of trying. Then you question the work involved and the rewards. So you withdraw. But don't be misled by the easy, do-nothing option: distress will appear like winter follows summer and down you will go. You can always choose correctly and positively: why go the opposite way? And you will choose correctly. Stress will not ruffle your feathers after this.

The scope of this chapter cannot address all the offsetting devices for stress, but there are many excellent books devoted to the subject. Tackling stress problems is similar to the business of goal achievement; in fact they are kin. You are learning to become an architect of your chosen future, and thereby a moderator of stress, whether associated with your goals or the inevitable stresses of life.

WHAT CAN YOU DO TO COMBAT DISTRESS?

In order to combat distress you might try relaxation techniques, physical exercise, structuring your time, eating correctly and developing a world view that is in harmony with life, not in opposition to it. Sounds straightforward, doesn't it? Supportive relationships (with a partner or friends) are important in the resistance and survival of stressful events; they should be nurtured throughout life (personal networking). Simple negative stress symptoms like arrogance, irritability, impatience and frustration can all be smoothed out by relaxing and disciplining your lower (unlikeable) self. If you're the steam-rolling, go-getting, aggressive burn-out type, *slow down* and set a level worth striving for, but short of perfection. Is an issue worth fighting for ... or are you heading for a stroke in proving some pathetic point? Keep cool, live a bit longer and enjoy your goals. The world should manage to rotate, even if you take a nap.

Burn-out is not the automatic result of certain events: it is the result of our *reaction* to those events. Burn-out is normally job-related (exhaustion, frustration, stagnation) but draws fuel from personal problems such as money, family and environment. 'Too much for too long' pushes the individual over the edge, depletes the resistance and adaptation store. Many of our personal goals may take care of distress, even burn-out. Write one now! For example: 'I will focus on the positive; I discover meaning in what I do; I take time to wind down; I apportion time for personal treats.' Perhaps your ultimate personal goal should be *self-acceptance and balance.*

You might not be at the burn-out point, but lesser distress might be more than enough for you. It's all relative. But there are so many simple things you might consider to reduce distress. Use your imagination! First of all, determine the sources of distress. Does it arise from people, career, family, finances or health? Once you have your starting point, you can come up with ideas to balance your situation. Frustration with young children can be offset by child-minders and time out, for example. Unsatisfactory family communication can be improved by a weekly at-home evening over a pleasant, unhurried meal. Financial worries can be tamed by systematic budgeting and self-restraint. Loneliness can be beaten by simply going out and circulating, or sharing your home with a student boarder. Work panics can be rewarded by do-nothing sessions with your feet up, drinking tea. 'Media depression' can be offset by avoiding TV, newspapers and current affairs fanatics. Feeling unfit (and worried about it) can be fixed by taking vitamins, exercising and visiting your doctor if necessary. The list is endless; the solutions must be yours. If you do nothing, distress may compound your problems. Recognize what's happening to you and plan your offsets, sometimes with pragmatism, sometimes with humour.

UNDERSTANDING DEPRESSION

Depression is an extension of distress, where the individual retreats from the world in order to achieve equilibrium. It happens to us all, more or less. Clinical depression that arises from suppressed anger and neurosis requires professional help, but that feeling of washed-out sadness is par for the course through our life episodes. Loss of some sort often triggers it: grieving, money, relationships, status, changes due to a health problem. Unresolved life crises, simmering conflicts, unfinished business and past disappointments all push emotions to physical expression in tiredness, loss of appetite, sadness and withdrawal.

The concept of desirable stress is of little interest to depressed people, for their minds are on other, internal things. In this state, self-worth usually evaporates, self-motivation and incentives to keep trying also disappear and goals are illusions. But this pattern can be understood. Rather than succumb to it, we can resist; not with force, but with insight. Just as stress can be used creatively, depression too may be positive: it can initiate a healing cycle. This is contrary to the popular view that we must rush to 'fix' all psychological low-spots and return to 'normal' immediately. We live in a self-deluding world of fast food, fast service and fast solutions. Many successful people have endured depression; sometimes it made them look at themselves even more deeply, enriching several dimensions of their lives in the process.

ACCEPTING DESIRABLE STRESS, DEFYING DISTRESS

All this business about becoming a self-aware Open Person should come into its own in defying distress. Can you see the link between stress, goals and the bigger picture – a determined, successful, holistic lifestyle? Setting goals which are not right for us, which either demand too little or too much and conflict with our unique personalities, will surely bring on unhealthy distress. But if you truly understand yourself and the reasons for your goals, you need not be anxious. You will have the right goals and you will have the right amount of desirable stress to accomplish them. Even if distress comes your way, you will understand what you must do to avoid trouble. Stay in control; you are gathering a fine set of tools to manage yourself and your future.

REVIEW

1 You have understood what stress is and accept its presence without fear.
2 You can discriminate between 'healthy' stress and 'unhealthy' distress; your approach to life events and change is more adaptive, less reactive.
3 Your pursuit of your goals is now an invigorating challenge, free of debilitating stress (distress).

11 The Tools in your Hands

Without tools man is nothing, with tools he is all.

Thomas Carlyle

OVERVIEW

We use tools to fashion both our needs and our intricate creations. People have excellent faculties (tools) within, but have forgotten how to use them. Our levels of consciousness (conscious and subconscious) are at our disposal. We achieve everything – from the mundane to the magnificent – in the mind. Accessing the power of the subconscious is our path to success. Learning how to harness this power is our central goal.

Silence and meditative techniques allow us to 'communicate' with ourselves. Practice in this enables us to suggest our goals to our higher level of consciousness. Then...we wait for results!

IMAGINATION, VISUALIZATION AND OTHERS...

What tools do we have? How can we begin to use them? Imagination, if you have it, is a good start – and we all like to believe we have it. Have you ever been amazed when sheer imagination solves a problem that wouldn't yield for you otherwise? Unfortunately, the conditioning process of life may have shrivelled this wonderful instrument of creativity. Too much imagination and you go insane (they say) or you live in a silly dream-like world of little practical value. Well, who has the final say? You have! Imagination is one tool in your kitbag. Visualization is another. Learning to use such tools and becoming an artisan takes perseverance. But cleaning, sharpening and trusting them each day requires love.

The tools are already inside you. Don't try looking outside, no matter what you think is out there. Your problem may be that you have lost contact with the things of value within you.

Are you an Open Person? When tools are placed in the Open Person's hands, the response is not 'What am I supposed to do with these?' but 'Show me how to use these to advantage.' Tools are sensitive instruments made for the job at hand. Treated properly, they can help you build wonderful things.

WHAT IS CONSCIOUSNESS?

Some understanding is required before getting to work. We have been focusing on your *consciousness* throughout the book, so let us begin our development there. Like most profound things, we seldom investigate what consciousness really is. Consciousness is an aspect of mind. It is the determination of reality, the knowledge of 'being'. It reflects the difference between illusion and reality. As thoughts and ideas arise in your mind, you recognize them. A thought without consciousness does not exist, but consciousness is always there (fortunately for us). Consciousness gives reality to your thoughts: it is reality. You are *really* sitting or standing here, reading these words. Words. You are *reading these words! Still reading these words...* Is your whole reality at this moment the words on this page? Or just the present reality which will disappear if the doorbell rings? Does your entire life and all its dimensions find its reality in the words of this page? Or does your mind think that your present activity has nothing to do with *you* at all?

The mind is a problem. We all have one, but we seldom make any serious attempt to learn how the thing works. We study books on car maintenance, breeding tropical fish and how the next generation of computers will change our lives; we learn the most taxing skills and adapt to incredible circumstances, but we pay marginal interest to the very apparatus that realizes all reality. In this chapter you are going to focus on that very apparatus and learn how it will open up your future.

WHAT IS YOUR MIND?

Is your mind just a big lump of cells up there, with various lobes and fissures? Just a well-ordered hierarchy of functional zones, controlling the motor responses, the senses and memory? Is the mind the anatomical unit within the skull or the storage capacity of the brain's various compartments? Does the medical profession understand what all the pieces of the brain really do?

Brain research has made significant progress, but only in recent years. Various studies into the active regions of the brain (through accident trauma, animal experiments and drug stimulation) have opened up uncharted territory. Growing interest in stress, fatigue, learning ability, memory and attitude has added to purely functional study, enabling integrated comprehension. So we can benefit from these investigations without saturating on medical or psychological jargon.

The brain has been investigated by several schools of analysis: traditional anatomy and physiology, psychology, psychotherapy, biofeedback, Gestalt and others. There is even a holographic theory of mind (multi-dimensional information storage and recall). It has always been clear that the brain is vast, with potential far beyond its everyday use, but little has been done to bring this to common knowledge. Yet why have such a marvellous system at our disposal and not use it to its full potential?

LEFT AND RIGHT BRAINS

One area of research that is gaining acceptance and being put to practical use is the left brain/right brain phenomenon. There are two cerebral hemispheres: left and right. They are physically distinct, though they have a cross-connection. The left hemisphere seems to prefer a certain range of ability and specialization. It is analytical, mathematical, decisive and intellectual. Language, reason, communication, leadership and order 'reside' in the left brain. The right hemisphere, meanwhile, is visual, visionary, intuitive, imaginative, childlike, spatial, creative, experimental, emotional and sensitive.

Of course, we get 'left or right dominant' people. Men tend to be left dominant, women right dominant, mostly through social conditioning. Western culture has generally favoured 'left' abilities as the 'true' success characteristics, considering the left strong and realistic, the right weak and idealistic. Eastern cultures are more spatial, spiritual and intuitive (right brained). At present, West and East are openly examining each other's characteristics, especially in the business sphere. The reason why the Japanese are so successful and Western intellect has failed to guarantee industrial supremacy is quite simply that the Japanese have been properly right-brained in their approach to business (i.e. visionary), while the West has been too left-brained (rational). In order to penetrate Western markets, the Japanese worked hard to understand the left brain characteristics of the West. And so they mastered the analytical, pragmatic, no-nonsense, organizational abilities, while still retaining their spatial, holistic base. The West is actually trying to work the other way: developing right brain skills to challenge the East!

OTHER POLARITIES: FEMALE, MALE

Japan found balance between left and right brain characteristics. In fact, Eastern cultures have long understood the human realm as essentially *two polarities*. Chinese culture talks of Yin and Yang, the two poles of human consciousness. Yin represents the female (dark, receptive, earth mother) and Yang represents the male (light, creative, heaven). In our left/right brain terms, Yin suggests the spatial, intuitive, sensitive nature, while Yang suggests the rational, analytical, intellectual one. According to Chinese philosophy, we are bi-polar: *we all possess female and male characteristics*. We think of 'the female' as nurturing, emotional and supportive and 'the male' as strong, providing and ambitious – that ties in with our conditioning – but the poles are ambiguous when we speak of shared characteristics within our given sexuality!

Carl Jung saw the same duality, the concurrent poles of masculine and feminine. He developed the concepts of *anima* and *animus*. Anima is the feminine element carried in a man's unconscious, while animus is the masculine element carried by a woman. We are conditioned to believe that men are tough, objective and ambitious, while women are soft, sentimental and intuitive. But Jung recognized that if we have a masculine and feminine side to our natures, then we cannot completely align ourselves to one pole or the other, even if it does suit society. So men *can* be gentle with children, cry over sad films and care for the welfare of others, while women *can* be business-like, highly intellectual and strong leaders. Both men and women have traits from the other poles. As an Open Person, you'll have to detach yourself from your conditioning and suppositions; you will then appreciate the big picture!

So the concepts of left/right brains, Yin/Yang poles and Jung's anima/animus connections are all very similar. Understanding these concepts may well tax your imagination, but acceptance will explain many unresolved issues and help you to grow in awareness. The Open Person should be able to grasp the significance of our male/female elements and still feel relaxed about being a man or a woman! Similarly, rigid thinking about left brain qualities being the only ones worth having must also be questioned. The scope of these ideas is too wide for this book, but I trust these pointers will prompt you to dig deeper.

A QUESTION OF BALANCE

To function as *complete* people, we must move towards balance – neither left nor right brain dominant, neither male nor female polarized. As thinkers, Einstein and da Vinci were all-rounders. They could dream and visualize like children (using the right brain), then *translate their imagination* into mathematical formulae, scientific concepts, mechanical devices or a Mona Lisa (left brain). When we refuse to dream a little, to imagine the future with us in it, we are switching off half our brain! Similarly, if you over-identify with your sexual stereotype (all-macho man or all-yielding woman), you will be limiting your life to one dimension. These are not some half-baked concepts from an obscure ivory tower: they are significant breakthroughs in understanding with practical value to our lives. Are you interested? Stay open.

Perhaps you are a left brain analytical type or a right brain creative type: what does that mean in terms of the mind?

NOT ONE MIND, BUT SEVERAL

You have three minds: *conscious, subconscious* and *overmind*. The one that you know best is the conscious mind. That handles most of the day-to-day organization of your life, solves basic problems and makes decisions logically. You are using your conscious mind to read and disseminate the words on this page.

Next is the subconscious mind. Most people have heard of this one, but know very little about it. Negative ideas are commonly formed about the subconscious, probably because of the association with mental health – we may avoid probing too much, in case our mind goes wobbly! Nevertheless, the subconscious looks after us like a good grandparent. It has certain magical qualities to it as well: intuition, creativity and inspiration.

The overmind is a projection of the subconscious mind, but may not be very active in most people. It is the highest level of mind that we humans possess. Telepathy and healing powers are some of its aspects, but people sometimes treat its faculties as a force of evil. Sixth sense, contact with the unknown and the occult appear threatening or intimidating to many people. So the overmind is considered a strange one, although it is so only if we treat it as such.

Beyond all 'mind' is the Overself. This deals with things of much higher purpose. For many people, the Overself is like a room in a house that has been locked up for decades – now and then a vague sense might remind us there's something of value in there. It is when we actively seek the spiritual aspects of our being that the Overself comes into play and becomes attuned within us. For our quest for ultimate truth goes beyond the mind. A person is free to choose how far the journey goes; for our purposes here, we shall go no further than the subconscious and the overmind.

The three minds exist together, with no natural conflicts between them, unless we stir things up. For most of the time, the conscious and the subconscious minds are the ones to concentrate on. The overmind may or may not be very 'active' in you, but as it is a projection of your subconscious, I shall from this point on refer to the subconscious mind as including the overmind.

It is useful to consider the 'mind' on two separate levels. This way, we can identify with its structure and understand how the respective minds work for us. The conscious mind is best imagined at the basal level, as it is used most commonly and directly. This is the 'mind' we loosely refer to all the time. It supports the next level, the subconscious mind.

The Overself perches (symbolically) on top, giving energy, as it were, to everything below. Think of the Overself as the sun in your inner galaxy; it is the very essence of ultimate wisdom in your life. To draw from that wisdom, you work through the subconscious.

It is essential to understand the way in which the mind functions in our lives. Without that understanding, you will not appreciate the power you have to change your life. I do not require you to become fluent in some academic abstraction – a working appreciation is enough. What is more important is the way in which you *exploit* the abstraction. In other words, don't get hung up on theories and concepts. Concentrate on de-mystifying the mind with a view to *practical* applications.

We will first consider the conscious mind on its own.

AN INFINITE SPACE AND RANDOM THOUGHTS

Have you ever been in a social group where the smokers gather at one point in the room? Have you noticed that an ashtray often sits under a table lamp? The smokers put their cigarettes there or wave them about under the catchment area of the lampshade. The smoke is drawn up into the mouth of the lampshade and the filaments of smoke arrange themselves into neat, ordered patterns. Since warm air rises, the filaments of smoke then ascend, through the warming effect of the light bulb. It is fascinating to study the emerging smoke patterns at the top of the lampshade. The filaments move through, sometimes straight and ordered, sometimes turbulent and chaotic. Some filaments mix and merge with others. They collide and disperse. Once clear of the lampshade, they flow into the room, becoming diluted and undetectable. There are even occasions when smoke will travel down the outside of the lampshade and re-enter at the bottom. This gives a truly hybrid stream of old and new smoke emerging at the top.

Consider the process. Try it, if you want to see things more clearly. Use more than one cigarette. Wave them about underneath the shade. Allow calm to establish itself and study the filaments of blue smoke rising from the outlet.

The lampshade and the smoke is a model of your mind. Watching the smoke emerging is like watching your mind. At the bottom, thoughts, moods, emotions, ideas, desires, feelings, truths and concerns enter the system. They are accelerated through, given a boost of energy to help them along. When they appear at the top, there they are again. If the air is still and no mixing takes place, the thoughts and everything else emerge intact. If you could cut a slice through the 'smoke' and look at it, you would see filaments like cells under a microscope. 'There's anger! Look, there's fear! There's lust!'

GOOD THOUGHTS, BAD THOUGHTS

So there you are, watching your mind at the top of a lampshade! And by doing things with the 'cigarettes' at the bottom, you can change the content of the 'mind' at the top. Some cigarettes might only produce 'good' thoughts, so light up a few and stick them in the ashtray. Witness lots of love, joy and trust at the top. Others only produce 'bad' thoughts. Light up for anger, frustration and fear. If you only light 'good' cigarettes, you will most likely conclude that your life is 'good' at the top end: 'I'm a happy person, because I have happy thoughts.' But if the smoke coming out is turbulent and upset, then there must be some 'bad' cigarettes there now!

Due to watching miserable smoke coming out, you may perceive that you are a basically miserable person. That is your impression of your mind, *your impression of self*, but it is not the 'real you'. It is really an example of taking yourself too seriously, allowing the 'self' to confuse miserable thoughts with the essential 'you'.

Your conscious mind is a *thought factory*, and the fascinating thing to grasp among the smoke is that *you have some control over your own thoughts*. Thought-discipline is a difficult skill to acquire, but if you become disenchanted with miserable thoughts, start consciously thinking happy ones! Your stomach is probably better served than your mind – if you cannot abide a certain food, you simply won't eat it. So why stuff negative thoughts in your head? Think positive thoughts, be a positive person!

WHAT VALUE THE THOUGHT?

To understand our minds, we need more than just a lampshade and a packet of cigarettes. The central issue is there, nonetheless: *Are those thoughts you, or are they just thoughts?* How should our consciousness relate to thoughts? Think about peeling potatoes with a sharp knife. The inevitable happens: you cut yourself. Think about the panicky feeling as you study the cut, waiting for the blood to stream out. Not a pleasant thought, was it? But have you become an unpleasant person all of a sudden, or a person scared to handle kitchen knives again? No. We think our thoughts, they pass through, they fade away, they are replaced by more, with anything remarkable being dispatched to memory for future reference.

So what is thinking? Thinking is a means of accessing information and processing it. Thinking is choosing between alternatives – wondering what that noise was, speculating on the outcome of a play, solving mathematical equations. Thoughts are relevant to you alone. Thoughts come and go…

THE CONSCIOUS MIND IS A CHATTERBOX

A wound-up mind is something like a hyperactive child after two bags of sugar – both a marvel and a pain in the neck. The mind rattles on, talking to itself, creating problems, solving problems. It *pretends* to be you, but it knows it isn't.

Your conscious mind must be kept in its place. It is a wonderful thing to be in possession of, but there is no need to follow every little game it decides to play with you.

The mind can easily become confused with identity or ego. People who are 'all ego' are very often those who 'function in the mind' –

for them, intellect rules. Precocious children (and adults) project ego by being oh-so-much smarter than everyone else. Being right is important to them, and teamwork is avoided, because their bright thoughts cannot dominate in a collaborative setting.

Good thinking, however, is not 'clever' thinking. Useful, brilliant thoughts are not mass-produced, egotistical and self-defensive thoughts! Thinking uses up energy and time; misappropriating these resources is unproductive and unwise. There is little ultimate satisfaction from ego-building. The conscious mind tends to be somewhat precocious, and not exactly wise. Wisdom is a more valuable commodity. I will show you why, and how you can develop it.

PROBLEM-SOLVING AND THE CONSCIOUS MIND

There is a tendency to entertain problems using only the conscious mind. This is rational enough, at least as a means of getting started. (Left brain characteristics are at play here.) Gathering the facts, analysing them, then acting on a decision is sensible logic. The bigger the problem though, the more data we tend to heap on. Analysis is the bread-and-butter of the conscious mind and, aware that it might get bogged down for want of information, the mind tells us to gather yet more data. So, rather than facing up to the problem, admitting the worst and accepting it, we often play games with data in our conscious mind. But procrastination and avoidance never solve problems, nor help us to plan our lives constructively.

So what is the way to tackle 'big' problems? Experts solve them by searching databases, conducting studies and retaining consultants who give objective appraisals of alternatives. Where computers are used, the solutions generated are assumed to be as right as solutions can possibly be: we load data which is right, so the solutions and the output scenarios must be right. Right? In such cases, people are definitely not operating on the basis of hunches. They are relying on pure and simple reason, and knowledge of the relevant facts. Beyond that, the processes of the conscious mind are mechanically applied to the exercise. Computers or consultants apart, the problems are tackled by the conscious mind.

But when we tackle our life problems and our goals, we seldom have the vast resources of corporate databases or consultants! The problems they are trying to wrestle with are usually different in any case. And the conscious mind and the exercise of reason are only ideal for certain types of problem. In fact, many of the character disorders and neuroses of our modern society stem from denying that problems exist at all, or refusing to deal with them. We leave the problems unsolved, but create a worse problem by becoming neurotic!

Sometimes the effects of our clumsy approaches to problem-solving are just as damaging. We can apply some of the methods used in the business world to our personal situations, providing we realize the limitations of reductionism which bedevil decision-making processes. But we need a system which integrates analytical methods with wisdom of a higher order.

THE SUBCONSCIOUS MIND IS MAGNIFICENT

This leaves us with the other mind of interest: the subconscious mind. What can it do for us? What power does it have? We could say that the subconscious is a medium for wisdom, although it is not wisdom itself. Wisdom is nothing like knowledge. Your conscious mind rattles along all day, dealing with knowledge in the form of thoughts and preparing thought groupings for memory. Facts, facts, facts. But where is the wisdom? The conscious mind is aware of itself, always proving its worth. The subconscious mind just is; it doesn't question everything, but does what it does very well. The real chance of making sense of knowledge lies within the subconscious mind. It is always at your disposal, 24 hours a day. But unless it is given instructions, it just plays second fiddle to your conscious mind.

Dreaming takes place in the subconscious mind. At that level of consciousness, you may fly above a city without an aircraft, suddenly find yourself talking to all manner of VIPs or experience bizarre episodes with steam trains, soldiers in the streets and you in your underwear. Despite the seemingly haphazard images of your dreaming mind, though, the analysis of certain significant events can tell a psychiatrist (and you) a great deal. Awake or asleep, your subconscious mind sees you as you really are, without disguises. Viewing yourself only with the conscious mind may be very limiting. Your subconscious knows you best.

KNOWLEDGE IS GOOD, WISDOM BETTER

We learn as we go, and some people believe they know it all – they are masters of the intellect. Talk to scientists – they will view life in generally scientific, functional, absolute terms. Similarly, a Paris pavement artist with talent, poverty and dreams will tell you he knows how things *really are*. Both are *victims* of their learning. Each has a personal world view, but there is nothing to say that either has *wisdom*. Their knowledge is nothing close to wisdom, neither wisdom of reality, nor wisdom of themselves. I want you to have knowledge, but *most of all* I want you to have wisdom.

In fact the knowledge and the learning we stuff into ourselves becomes a handicap in many ways. It tends to overwhelm and ridicule any other forms of consciousness and somehow it fails to satisfy. If our world view (based on our learning and our progressive conditioning) tells us the world is a horrible place, then ideas to improve one tiny aspect of it may become absurd to us. 'No room for silly, soft ideas here!' *Don't rely on all that knowledge inside you.* It might be impressive at cocktail parties or in your learned circles, but give it only nodding respect. Keep an open mind about other, more satisfying and powerful possibilities.

THE GATEWAY TO YOUR BEST FUTURE

Your subconscious mind is your gateway to insight, intuition and real wisdom. It is your friend, your mindful guardian. It warns you of danger and helps you through difficult times. *It is a magic force within you, available and willing to help, always. Whatever honest goal you assemble in your conscious mind, the subconscious mind can help you to achieve it, solve it or create it.* The subconscious mind never goes to sleep, nor does it ignore you if it gets tired (it never gets tired). Ask it for something and it listens. Your conscious mind is good at puzzles and IQ tests, but try asking it to *really* help you! But your subconscious mind can do this, for it knows you best and it watches over events. In fact it is taking note of what you are doing right now. Perhaps it was your subconscious mind that instructed you to buy this book and get started on your new life!

People who take charge of their lives learn to access their subconscious mind. They discover the practical value of a focused life, accessing real wisdom instead of facts, figures and idle thoughts. They learn to see the world and their place in it rather differently. There is nothing new in this, nothing strange or threatening either. *You can do it too.* You have energies and powers that you have unconsciously subdued over the years. The conditioning processes of life, from learning how to use the toilet properly to preparing yourself for an interview, have forced any 'unusual' practices out. So you must rediscover the very things you were urged to remove. Integrating abstract concepts into your everyday routine is far from easy, but then nothing worthwhile ever is.

People speak of 'unlearning' as the true path to learning: in order to rise above the ordinary, you must unlearn the things that bind you, and learn those which will make you great.

SUBCONSCIOUS SERENDIPITY

Access to the subconscious allows us to gainfully harmonize the two levels of mind directly available to us and simultaneously integrate the benefits of left and right brain characteristics. It is a focusing technique, consolidating vast areas of consciousness and awareness into a manageable form. Reaching far beyond the here-and-now immediate, it is something like the ability to recall 'interesting' dreams at will. How often have we been frustrated by whispers from fascinating dream-voyages, lost forever in the subconscious? We can do great things in our dreams... The waking state has too many restrictions. Yes, and we put them there! But we can take steps to remove them!

When the conscious and subconscious minds work together, with mutual respect for each other, the phenomenon of a 'new person' transformation becomes possible. Serendipity then enters the picture in a new, exciting way. Rather than 'other people' having 'all the luck', we begin to see that serendipity is available to all, but only if we reach out and make use of it. The subconscious knows serendipity well; the conscious mind does not.

WARNING: NEGATIVE AND POSITIVE THEMES

The subconscious, however, has a negative aspect, which should be explained at this point. Although the subconscious mind desires to be your guide and inner strength, paradoxically it also has the capacity to frustrate and actually harm you. Since it has no reasoning ability of its own, it is apt to treat all incoming messages as equal entities. Thus, if your boss or teacher dresses you down in a passionate tantrum of criticism, the subconscious assumes it's all true! If your self-esteem and conscious mind are off guard, you store the message deep in your subconscious and an unconscious feeling of inadequacy is created. So many of our phobias, hidden fears and personality problems stem from this aberration. Just as we can implant positive suggestions, we can also cultivate negative ones. Take care.

Awareness of this leads to a precious truth: if we can search out and replace 'wrong' themes in our subconscious with 'right' themes, we can look forward to better lives. Learning how to direct the childlike, unquestioning nature of the subconscious is essential. The conscious mind will guide you in that task. This is where the two minds working in harmony form a powerful combination. The *impressionable subconscious*, coupled with the *reasoning conscious*, gives you the best of both worlds – a fully integrated 'mind system'.

SILENCE AND PEACE: YOUR CREATIVE SPACE

Sceptical people will find this all quite absurd. *Everything is absurd to some people* (not to you I hope). *Stop listening to them. Listen to yourself!* More things exist than can be defined by logic. This is what you will appreciate here.

How can you listen to yourself? First of all, *believe in belief* as a practical concept of growth consciousness. Believe that what you need is *inside* you, and you will learn how to access it. No voice will physically speak, but the information you need will be decanted into your conscious mind for you to act upon. The subconscious mind carefully assembles the right guidance and the conscious mind acts as an interface with you. You can readily perceive the conscious mind, but the subconscious is hidden out of the present and must be accessed by protocol. Learning the basics of that protocol is the task at hand; there is no other way to the wisdom you require.

The best place to listen is in a quiet environment. Many people avoid the uncanny atmosphere of silence and solitude. It worries them, threatens them. They must be around active people, TV and hi-fis. They must speak, feeling that silence in company signifies disapproval, perhaps a hint of finding others shallow. They allow torrents of noise to destroy their peace; they talk for hours with no particular focus or purpose, with no real communication. But real silence and solitude are essential for the subconscious mind to function. It is a sad reality of our society and civilization that we act as if we are working to escape from ourselves. We consciously or unconsciously pollute our creative space with junk, as if there is something to be feared in there! Why do that? I am sure you will think carefully about this. You will desire peace to focus on your goals in life, rather than fill in time in the amusement arcade of aimless distraction.

Silence abounds on hill-tops, deserted beaches or in caves. Sitting in a rowing boat out on a lake is an excellent place for silence. You can also find silence in an empty room, in the early morning, even in the heart of a city. Silence. Frightening to some. Self-challenging, intimate. But if you are going to make progress, *you must find a silent space.*

When you have found your silent place, go to it as often as you can. You should try to have some truly silent time every day. You must not have a radio or other distraction at your side. *The whole point of silence is to be utterly alone with the little ears and voices inside your subconscious mind* – they will not make the effort to communicate with you if you're tapping your toes to some other beat.

I should be open with you and explain what you are practising here. It is essentially meditation – without incense, candles or chanting! Meditation is a well-established means of settling your conscious mind and moving through to the higher levels. It might sound weird to you if you've never meditated before. But then you did say you were an Open Person now.

SILENCE AND THE SUBCONSCIOUS MIND

This exercise introduces practical methods which will help you re-establish contact with your own subconscious. You must be in a silent environment, with no chance of casual disturbance. Pressures of time and everyday concerns must be absent.

SILENCE

Sit on a chair, on the floor or upright in bed, keeping your spine straight. You don't have to be a Yoga Master to perform this exercise, just be relaxed. Immerse yourself in the quiet of the room. Be aware of your inner doubts about this strange practice. Look about you and carefully study each familiar object that your gaze rests upon. Let the usual pattern of thoughts carry on as before. Don't worry that you're not taking this seriously enough. Your conscious mind loves new things, it's having a new experience and it will want to give a running commentary on this funny thing you're doing. All the while, try to lose focus on strong, dominating thoughts: treat them with courtesy, but don't let them chatter at you.

Your conscious mind will be highly excited at first, but as you adjust to the environment of calm, it will slow down somewhat. After some minutes, begin sensing your breathing. Breathe in, breathe out, breathe in, breathe out – slow, deep breaths. Keep your attention fixed on your own breath. Feel it entering and leaving your body. Sense the physical and auditory sensations as it passes through your nostrils or your mouth. Feel your chest rising and falling. Your silent space, your breath, your life. Thoughts will float about, but return your focus to the breathing process. Imagine that each breath calms you down more and more.

After a few minutes, divert your attention to your eyes. Keeping your head horizontal, roll the eyes upwards. Try to gaze through your eyebrows. Blink only if you must; try to keep the fixed gaze if you possibly can. Your eyelids will become progressively tired and you will want to close your eyes. If they reopen, look up as before. Eventually your eyes will close. Opening them will seem like too much effort, too much bother. This voluntary submission will relax your entire body. Don't fight the relaxation, simply enjoy it. Settle down comfortably, but don't go to sleep. Allow yourself to drift into a state of quiet but conscious relaxation. Study the little thoughts streaking through your mind like smoke filaments from a lampshade. Look at the thoughts as they drift up, then allow them to disperse into the room. You are meditating.

There is no right or wrong way to reach a state of calm well-being. Some people like a lit candle before them to set the mood; that's fine. If you consciously try to fight the process, you'll never get very far into it, nor will you reap the ultimate benefits. If your mind is in a cynical, doubting, self-defeating mode, you may have to try again later. Allow time for the smoke to clear! Your thoughts may all be bad today! Your first sessions may seem a waste of time, but at least they prepare you for better. Don't give up. This isn't easy, but attitude, belief and tenacity are essential.

By shutting out the chatter and gossip of the conscious mind, it is possible to hear the inner voices, 'whispers', from the subconscious. Conversely, your subconscious will be able to hear you. It is as simple as that. Listening is the skill to grasp here, not some trick of dredging up inspired thoughts from the deep. Your conscious mind will be teasing you and laughing at you whenever you go to meditate. But persevere: you are not your conscious mind!

On this exercise, you are not looking for any great manifestations from your subconscious; you are merely trying to experience what silence and self-contact really are. No doubt you will notice curiosity building up and experience the urge to go further next time. There is a pleasant calm and strength in 'listening to the silence'. It seems to achieve nothing on the face of it. But patiently, respectfully, stay open to what you see and feel in that silent space. Everything is relevant – even the trashy thoughts that whizz about, the noises you may hear outside.

DEEP SILENCE

This is simply a more developed state which follows the silence and relaxation established earlier. It needs only time and continuing calm to come about. Here, you will have managed to put your conscious mind into neutral for most of the time. Odd thoughts will come and go. Some will linger, asking for attention. Old worries, old amusements, old friends, old enemies... Give them a respectful wave and see them on their way. At this stage, you will consider your thoughts to have validity, but much less impact on your overall present-consciousness. In fact, this is a simple confirmation of having reached deep silence through straightforward meditation. You will also experience a feeling of well-being, a comfortable state between blissful sleep and focused awareness.

In deep silence, you find your breathing much more interesting than anything in the mind. Thoughts still come and go, but they cannot drag your attention away from the breath for very long. A deeper calm will arrive for you. Random thoughts will become less interesting and less intrusive at this point. You consciously begin to ignore them. They cannot command your interest any longer! You have your thoughts but they don't have you! This deeper calm approximates to a trance state induced through self-hypnosis. The hypnotic state is under your direction: you are the master and the subject. Don't feel anxious about losing control. If the doorbell rang, you'd be quite aware. You cannot become hung-up in this state; the natural tendency is to come out of hypnosis or simply snooze and then wake up.

At this point, mere thoughts are secondary to the greater awareness that you have created for yourself. You are aware of your breath, aware of yourself and generally much less focused on thoughts forever moving about. You will begin to revel in the silence. You might find yourself patting yourself on the back and saying how smart you are − but that is your conscious mind, your ego, slipping a little vain thought in! Recognize it as such and go back to the tranquillity again. Not only do you have calm: you have control.

It is in this wonderful state of calm that we can watch the mind. Just as you imagined you were watching the mind when observing smoke going through a lampshade, here you are conscious of watching the vast open space of your actual mind. You have put thoughts where thoughts belong. You appreciate the mind for what it is. It is less threatening to you now, less intimidating, less limiting. It doesn't throw worries or anxieties at you. It doesn't demand undivided attention to the relentless internal dialogues going on in the conscious mind. *Rather than losing your mind, you have found it!*

At this stage, the subconscious mind is *available to you*. The conscious mind is there all right, but in a safe state of calm. It has become sluggish in manufacturing thoughts. It no longer has the energy to fire thoughts into the general consciousness, like a child thrusting toys at you, wanting to play. In fact, the conscious mind is rather *enjoying* this little break you have given it. (This is how many burnt-out people regain balance: they need to give their conscious minds some rest and recreation.)

Coming out of a session is easy. Rather than immediately rising as if nothing had happened, follow a procedure that suits you. For example, think to yourself, 'That was a good session. Next time will be even better. I'm nicely relaxed, refreshed. I feel good. When I open my eyes, I'll be recharged, calm and happy.' Smile, and resume your chores of the day.

GOALS AND THE SUBCONSCIOUS

Talking and relating to your subconscious mind is the very process by which you can make some sense of your mind and your life. Wisdom is in there, if you can be bothered to uncover it. Visit your subconscious mind a few times before asking things of it. Show some respect. Do you borrow things from new neighbours as soon as you meet them? You may have to practise many times, but familiarity and patience will help. Eventually you will reach the desired state of calm in a matter of five minutes. You may feel that you have not achieved the 'depth' required, but actually you will be surprised how little depth is enough.

Now you have some ideas on the technique of accessing your subconscious mind, it is necessary to learn the best ways in which you can approach it and ask for help. Meanwhile, it is imperative that you become familiar with silence and with the workings of your two minds. Don't just accept what you are being told. Seek it out for yourself, prove it and continue to believe in it. In this regard, practise the meditation exercises until they become part of your daily activities. Consider them to be just as vital to your well-being as good food and exercise. Learn to enjoy these sessions. Look forward to them. Never consider them as intrusions on your time or sanity. Don't treat them as a peculiar experiment that you are merely observing with your ego!

YOU CAN BRING OUT YOUR GOALS NOW

Interesting as it might be, the study of the mind is not the purpose of this book. Let's return to the goals you set yourself earlier. Your subconscious mind can be applied to achieving those goals.

Assemble your goals, and become intimately familiar with them. If you have too many, limit them to a number you can cope with. You have been through the mind-exercises of visualizing your goals both before and after they were in finished form. So, in a subtle way, you have already introduced the goals that matter to your subconscious mind, via the analytical conscious mind. Accordingly, you need not worry that all this is going to be a shock to the system. In fact, your subconscious may have helped you to select your goals, winnowing out the wheat from the chaff. You may not have been aware of its silent urging.

Visualize your goals whenever you have a day-dreaming moment. Don't wait until you meditate. Visualization keeps the goals fresh in your consciousness, so you are *always aware of what you want to do*. The achievement of goals is a *constant* sport of the mind, so keep the ball in play. Visualization is ideal for the subconscious: a picture has more meaning than pages of words.

WATCH YOUR PROTOCOL

When you have a meditation session, you can take one of your goals in with you. That doesn't mean reading out the entire goal to your subconscious, saying, 'OK, that's it. I want this by 5 o'clock on Thursday.' Have the content of the goal in short-form, easily remembered and visualized. You do not need to prepare special words for your subconscious. It knows what you mean. Single words will often be enough and visual translations will then take over. If you have prepared beforehand, the goals will be fresh in your memory. A clear visual image is better than words, if you are good at calling up images in this way.

Once you have completely established your deep silence, *make your subconscious mind aware of the goals you want to see fulfilled. Just consciously think the goals in there and leave them alone.* Share the problem or the dream with your subconscious, and see your goal in finished form.

Every time you have a session, review your goals beforehand and offer them up during the session. You are simply consulting your own subconscious mind in order to jointly manage the business of realizing goals. The only requirement is that the consultation be carried out in a state of inner calm. Your subconscious always respects your attention to such details of protocol and will reward you with results.

MATERIAL GOALS: A CAUTION

You might think it ridiculous to say 'I have a Jaguar XJS Convertible, white with red seats.' Material goals are not in the present reality, although I urged you to state them this way. That is the problem of dealing with the new while the old is still firmly in place. With personal goals, there is no problem: self-suggestion impresses the subconscious, displacing the negative themes you had collected. Material goals need some additional care.

Visualize the completed material goal as a consequence of definition, a reality which you are attaining with the help of your subconscious. As explained earlier, the subconscious tends to accept messages as true and totally valid. If you can learn to harmonize the conscious mind to your meditation, you can use both minds to make sense of the anomaly and project the material goal in such a way that the subconscious realizes the XJS has still to be found!

SHARE THE GOALS AND WAIT

Once the goals have been shared, there is nothing more to do but wait. Some of the things you have asked may not be straightforward. These will require time and the required effort. But be careful – the subconscious has a very poor sense of time. Your conscious mind is the one watching the clock. Both minds have to become synchronized: if you don't specify some form of schedule, you might get what you want, but much too late! You will have to use the conscious mind to 'pace' requests and directives to the subconscious.

Your subconscious mind will be aware of what you want and will begin looking for opportunities on your behalf. When there is something that will help you, the subconscious mind will lead you right to it. It will also make you open and focused enough to see possibilities beyond your immediate perception. We refer to this process as 'mental set'. You become attuned to specific things. For example, if your best friend owns a blue car, then you look twice at every blue car. Successful athletes talk of the 'inner game', where visualization and mental set focuses performance. The same methodology applies to stress reduction and avoiding psychosomatic illness – 'mind over matter', if you like. *What you think, you get; what you believe, you achieve.* This acute sense will not be obvious at first, especially if you are suspicious of the relaxation/self-contact process. Apply yourself to the silence from which all these things grow and suspend idle judgement. Learn to trust yourself and your methods. The benefits of realizing your goals are surely worthwhile, aren't they?

You may already appreciate that meditation can be used to establish inner calm and promote a sense of wholeness. If there are opportunities for you to join a meditation group, by all means join it. You don't have to be the 'type' to do such things. Where is the Open Person now? Meditation is a singularly powerful tool in understanding the mind and the potential levels of consciousness that we humans have. *And that means all humans, not just fortunate ones.*

METHOD FIRST, THEN RESULTS

The meditation method used here is structured around achieving results. There is no attempt at realizing higher, spiritual things. Nevertheless, it trains you in the *discipline of mindfulness*. It gives you a focal point you perhaps never thought existed. When you become aware of yourself in this special way, the impossible becomes more and more possible. For a change, the mind becomes a *listening* entity, rather than a *chattering* one.

By willingly sharing your goals with those little ears beyond the gossip, you get the support, the advice and the guidance you need to achieve your goals. Perhaps you had goals before, but without a point of focus, they scattered to the winds. *Now you have that point of focus,* that central space which welcomes your goals and intensifies your desire to see them achieved.

During and after meditation, certain clarifications will surface. Strong urgings will direct you in particular ways, when the time is right. You may receive powerful, conscious thoughts which suggest alternatives or fresh insights. Direct commands may come: 'Go and build your house...you can do it...the money is not an issue.' Then again, a string of silent sessions may appear to produce nothing. The time is not ripe. Then one day in the garden, driving along late at night or day-dreaming in a crowded shop, the idea pops into your head! First thing in the morning is a common time for eurekas. Your subconscious mind never sleeps, remember?

Don't expect a step-by-step directive to achieving every goal. Remain flexible and let things work out as they will. The actual form of manifestation will vary from person to person.

ACTING ON THE PROMPTINGS

When you begin to sense the feedback from your subconscious, don't get haughty and decide 'you' know better. Do you really know better than the deep wisdom accessed through your subconscious? If you think so, reread 'The Open Person' (Chapter 2) and give yourself a second chance!

Signals, help, advice and instructions from your subconscious mind are there for you to use. Exercise discretion to defer action, if sudden application of the directive would be inappropriate, but don't snub your own subconscious by deferring all the directives! Don't try modifying or conditioning the ideas either. Why condition messages when you sought unconditioned help in the first place? An insight may come up which is general, requiring some interpretation and shaping. So use your judgement, but don't design a square wheel.

ONGOING EXERCISES SHARPEN FOCUS

Throughout the practice of communicating with your subconscious mind, you must continue with some less heady exercises:

- Read your list of goals out loud to yourself every day. Read them slowly, deliberately, and learn them by heart for your meditations. As you read them, imagine you are already with your goals. See them, feel them, visualize them completely finished.
- See yourself as the person you want to be. Go about each day as if you *are* the person. It sounds like acting out a role, but it's a dress rehearsal for the person you are growing into. Take this exercise seriously.
- Before you meditate, have your goals ready in your conscious mind. Take a moment to impress your consciousness with the business at hand. It makes life easier for you in the middle of a wonderfully calm and productive session.

If your goals are real and reasonable to you, they will be real and reasonable to both levels of your mind. You must then work with your subconscious mind in the proper way: in silence. Gentle coaxing begins the process; respectful attention to the promptings completes it. When the 'little voices' give you the clues and the directives, heed them. That is the way to realize your true capabilities.

REVIEW

1 You have called up creative forces within you by understanding how the mind functions. Myths about the mind have been dispelled. You are under no illusions regarding the limited faculties of the intellect.

2 You have discovered how to access your subconscious mind and realize the power that lies within you, waiting to be utilized.

3 You have learned how to reach a state of inner calm and feel very close to your creative centre.

4 Your programme of goal achievement is focused in your subconscious.

PART 4
What is Missing?
Are you Ready for Success?

FORWARD PASSAGE...
FROM NEGATIVE...
                 TO POSITIVE

'I've got problems, underneath the surface. Maybe we all need psycho-therapy. But digging all that junk out would spoil everything for me.'

'To be complete, I must look at the whole person, not just the favourable parts.'

'A goal of travelling to China is realis-tic, but accepting my son's drug addic-tion is absurd, even if he is reformed now.'

'Self-development means accepting reality and allowing light into dark corners.'

'It's all too good to be true. I follow the arguments, but I'll drift along, thank you.'

'I find new truths in all arguments and resolve to profit from them.'

'Success? I still can't put my finger on it.'

'I have a clear view of what success is for me.'

12 The Goals You Avoided

It is only because of problems that we grow mentally and spiritually. It is through the pain of confronting and resolving problems that we learn.

M. Scott Peck

OVERVIEW

We all have suppressed desires, ambitions or embarrassing areas of our lives which need some attention. If we refuse to acknowledge them, we might not achieve the quality of success and harmony which is best for us.

There is little point in avoiding 'problem goals' if so doing will make us vaguely dissatisfied or distracted. But we can write goals to resolve unpleasant episodes in our lives or unblock burning ambitions.

YOUR UNWANTED GOALS

When drawing up your list of goals, there must have been some you discarded as ridiculous or trivial. No doubt you weeded out those that made the list look greedy or unmanageable. How can a person focus on 20 or 30 goals? Even 10 goals can make you very busy. But then, if you believe your list is absolutely complete, you are either a truly Open Person or you are prone to deceiving yourself!

One possible reason you missed some goals is fear of other people seeing them. Another could be that you do not want to see them.

WHAT GOALS COULD THESE BE?

When we dig deeper, there are usually some darker sides to our nature which we decline to own, or something that blocks a constructive idea, denying its potential to help us. Did you discard such goals as overcoming a roguish temper, wanting to give money to a good cause, realigning yourself with abandoned or rejected spiritual beliefs or reconciling yourself with a wayward daughter or a bullying father?

Relationships and matchmaking is an area of concern for many. This is a complex area, of interest to married couples and long-term lovers as well as lonely hearts. Too many people just drift, experiencing a vague sense of dissatisfaction with a current relationship or the loneliness of being a single in a couples' world. They think the perfect combination will 'happen' one day, but are frustrated when it never does. It is often a case of sights being set too high, or conversely, of being too indiscriminate and acting before thinking at all. Both courses lead to trouble. The 'married at 23, divorced at 33' cycle shows that many people traditionally satisfy social and ego pressures before determining what they really want from life. Although a formalized relationship may have been 'right at the time', people often blossom as individuals *after separating*.

Everyone not already settled in the 'perfect relationship' generally wants to meet the ideal soul-mate, unless they have consciously opted to be independent (and there's nothing whatsoever wrong with that). But there is an element of self-motivated destiny in meeting the *right* person, rather than *one that will do*! The best partnerships generally evolve from mutual attraction, *shared values* and a growing state of harmony. The ideal relationship is not what romantic idealism or fashion decides; it is totally individual and personal. Write a goal to achieve the relationship you dream of: 'I want a loving, committed relationship in my life, with the person I know is right for me.'

Other 'difficult' goals, related to this, are sexual ones, such as secretly wanting to 'let go', to gain the confidence to discuss things openly with a partner, to feel uninhibited when exchanging ideas on technique, to dispel the stereotypes of male/female roles and myths in order to be sexually mature...

You may also have taboo goals related to very low self-esteem or personal inadequacy. You might have decided, in some anguish, that you need a nose or an ear job. That's too expensive or silly! People would laugh. Yet people will laugh when you have a funny nose *and* after it's fixed – that's people! If you feel a shapelier nose would help you, then it's a goal, so waste no time in declaring it a goal!

Then there may be things in your past that haunt you. So your 'problem' goal might be to think the issue through and reach a better understanding or solution. Perhaps you need to consult a counsellor or psychotherapist, but your goal could be to explore the problem on your own first.

Avoiding a problem altogether just creates more complex problems. Why have all the trappings of the good life, but suffer misery from neuroses? Facing such problems should be less intimidating than previously — you have a system to help you now.

AVOID INAPPROPRIATE AND SELF-DEFEATING GOALS

Some goals shoot themselves. For example: 'My problem is too big to be solved.' Oh yes? The can't-get-there-from-here syndrome... Another is the goal of the dedicated martyr: 'I really want to get out of the rat race and live off the land somewhere in the mountains, but my wife hates hardship and my two kids are happy in their school...' Then there is the diametric dreamer, always wanting to prove the world wrong: 'You say you can show me how to run my own airline or become a leading model, but you know I'm only a butcher from a small town and all I can do is saw chops!' This brings up the question of the possible versus the impossible. Don't keep painting yourself into corners by being either too humble or excessively ambitious. Choose the right goals, visualize the possibles and believe in them!

One other goal form that causes people some concern is the 'if only' variety. These are goals in suspension, wishful thinking with no hope or intent of action: if only you had done or had not done something... We love to keep past mistakes with us, but they are long gone, washed out to sea, dissolved to ions. They are not part of your future.

Why not get your 'problem' goal roughly sorted out, no matter how confused you are? Then, if it's appropriate, talk to your confidante, without being too specific at first. That family might find the simple, wholesome life in the mountains ideal; they might welcome Daddy leading them out of the rat race and chain stores. We all get trapped in our collective roles. Remember, if you haven't a proposition, you can't talk it over or expect a response.

DIFFICULT GOALS: AREAS TO CONSIDER

Here's a synopsis of likely problem areas for your immediate reference:

Excessive Personality or Behaviour
   Anger and violence.
   Abrasive characteristics.
   Self-persecution, including self-inflicted anxiety.
   Hyperactivity, leading to burnout.
Relationships
   Splitting up with a partner.
   Containment or grounding of animosities.
   Sexual maturity.
Spiritual Issues
   Answering a call to higher purposes.
   Lack of Information
   Pressures of popular opinion, consensus.
   Fear, guilt, misconceptions.
Reconciliatory Problems
   Parental, children (past unpleasantness).
   Friends or business partners (betrayal, conflict).
   Parties to accidents or tragic experiences.
Disapproval of Material Goals
   Partner or family causing guilt complex.
   Fear of extravagance with no responsibility.
   Moral or religious shadow.

DARK DOORS, UNEASY SHADOWS

You will recognize the doors you would rather not enter. And the more difficult your problems or schemes, the more sensitive you are going to be about facing them. But coming to terms with the impossible/possible dilemma is the first hurdle. With that out of the way, you will muster energy for the rest. Many goals will require hard work and dedication (a weekly 'deep silence' is not enough). But you will grow into your goals; they are not too big if you chose them wisely.

   Do exercise painful experiences on paper. Bring it all out; it is excellent therapy. Bring out anger, disgust, shame, panic. Set up a dialogue with yourself to place the facts in front of you, then examine your feelings and possible paths forward. If you desire growth, suffer a little, then take heart and move on. Follow this with an Open Person's resolve to structure a goal to help you deal with it. Here are some examples:

Reconciliatory Problems

Background

My partner had an affair with someone at work. I couldn't understand why at the time: we had everything going for us. We were finally seeing returns for all the hard work we put into our home and we had overcome various setbacks together. I could sense vague changes in our relationship, but to raise the issue seemed pointless. I didn't want to know the truth, I suppose. When I noticed more positive signs, I decided to set the trap. It was easy. It seemed peculiar, funny almost, seeing a stranger being so familiar with a person you had trusted for 12 years.

We separated for a year (the affair collapsed after three weeks). On the surface I took it all very well, but deep down, it broke my spirit. But then, I see this soap-opera fling as a comedy of errors, rather than a kick in the teeth. Part of me wants to try again.

I think I was obsessed then with money, status, furniture, a second car, the home electronics, the exotic holidays. That's what I thought we both wanted. We did set out loving each other; what else is there? I hadn't considered that merely gathering possessions and affording the things money will buy doesn't make a marriage. Maybe there's a chance to forgive – my partner, for the betrayal; me, for my insensitivity about our roles in the marriage.

Goal

I have met my partner and have spent the entire day talking things through, at a place we both like. We were both open, and kept our minds on the future, not the past.

We have reached a common understanding, after discussing what we both want from our relationship. We will make the decision to continue our marriage and to learn from our experience.

Spiritual Issues

The Billy Graham Crusade was in town. Last time I meant to go, but didn't. This time I thought I might go, but couldn't get motivated. Then my curiosity won: what drew people to see him?

It was frustrating in the downtown traffic, near the stadium. Parking was another headache. I walked along a side street to join the slow mass of people on their way to the stadium. Time was moving on. Dodging around people, I made some headway, but doing so was difficult and irritating.

A 'Don't Walk' signal stopped the flow of pedestrians. One car sounded its horn to clear the busy junction. It added to my sense of rising tension. A badly-crippled man blocked my way to the kerb; his sticks were a nuisance. He would certainly slow everyone down. I drew level with him, one of his sticks touching my left shin. I was hot and bothered. I bet Billy Graham didn't arrive like this!

Suddenly I felt that strange sense of presence you get when someone won't take their eyes off you. The fellow was staring at me. He was about 20, handsome, athletic looking, but hopelessly immobile without sticks. He wore a leather bomber-jacket, an Eric Clapton tee-shirt, designer jeans and training shoes. The sticks seemed like a joke; they just didn't fit. All the while, he was looking at my tense face, relaxed, gentle, full of concern, smiling.

'Going...to...see Billy Graham?' I blurted, worried by his eyes.

'Yeah, that's right. I'm going. We're all going to see Billy Graham,' he replied, as if he had the reply ready.

When the light changed, he called out to everyone 'OK, here we go!' and we all moved forward like children on an outing with teacher. I walked at his pace, one of his sticks slapping my leg. We didn't speak, but I'd look at him now and then. There was always the calm smile, the penetrating eyes. His motion was difficult, excessive, an embarrassing spectacle. We parted company at the turnstiles. Handicapped people, Gate K; people like me, any other gate.

Inside, I tried to take it all in. The sound wasn't too good, but then the stadium was built for sports fixtures and rock concerts. I suppose it was just as I expected. When people 'went forward' to commit their lives, I asked myself if I could really do that. Wasn't it just good old American evangelism at its best, getting the better of the masses? I sat and observed, seeing the show out. Wheelchairs were pushed to the front and the prayer began. I closed my eyes. It was silent apart from the prayer, with a dull, repetitive noise, barely audible, in the background. Air conditioning perhaps. I opened my eyes, looked down, and saw the young man making his lonely way to the front. I watched him, calmly, smiling, feeling close to him, tears streaming down my face. I can't remember anything Mr Graham said that night. But then my lesson walks with me all my life, one stick slapping my leg to remind me.

Spiritual matters are awkward to deal with in a generally unspiritual social consensus. Unfortunately, this has meant that our spiritual side is rarely talked about or disclosed in everyday circles. In a world which largely celebrates the intellect, reception of such matters is often critical or hostile. So when a person feels the need to express inner consciousness of a spiritual nature, there are very few outlets which welcome any sharing. It really has become a personal affair.

But we are not just molecules and electricity. If you want personal spiritual development, don't be ashamed to include goals directly related to your own spiritual growth. Please do not demand visions or miracles within this context! But do consider the goal-setting process a suitable vehicle for focusing these very personal wishes.

Another familiar but 'difficult' personal goal area, as mentioned earlier, is the field of sexuality. And although it is not the intention of this book to solve the sex problems of the nation, it is only appropriate that some attempt is made to address this one. The Open Person and the issues of sexuality are indeed an interesting combination. Our social consensus has changed (so we are told), and being open is the key to coping with it all. At least, we can be open relative to our own consciousness. So choose your own way, not that of popular consensus, or the hype of promotional conditioning. An excellent reference work, with no reservations and great respect, is *The Hite Report* by Shere Hite (*Female Sexuality*, Macmillan, New York, 1976; *Male Sexuality*, Macdonald, London, 1990). Ms Hite blazed new trails by basing her work on extensive matter-of-fact questionnaires and well-ordered replies from respondents. This is especially important, as there are enough distortions and half-truths out there to make you feel you have serious problems! Be aware of that, and be free to make constructive goals in this area, like any other.

Sexual Maturity
Background
We had a good marriage until recently. I have worked for the last two years, wanting an interest outside the home. Often my husband and I are both tired after a working day. He joined a sports club six months ago, and since then he has steadily believed he is becoming inadequate as a lover. More and more, he pushes the problem to the background. Whenever we do begin something, he becomes self-critical and everything stops. His point of reference is the macho-image of his club friends, I'm sure. He takes their shallow stud mentality too literally, and seems to be measuring his 'performance' against their innuendo. He won't discuss it. He's ashamed and scared. I know that men have this performance thing, even an underlying fear of women, if they can't be in control. I can see it's a vicious circle.

Our relationship is deteriorating fast. We both avoid the problems by working more. We keep off the topic of sex to maintain the status quo. It's a tidy but useless solution. I haven't stopped loving him. How can I reassure a man who feels he is no good if he can't perform as his friends say he should? We're in this together, and I want to help him through it.

Goal
I am patient and supportive with my husband, and always find ways of removing the pressures he places on himself. I am resourceful and sensitive in our love making, replacing performance as an objective with fun and relaxation.

I am aware that as the pressures to perform are removed from our physical relationship, we will develop a closer, more open and more mature marriage.

THE BIGGER PICTURE

You can now appreciate what it means to be an Open Person. If you are to make real progress, you should add those 'awkward' goals to your list. Think about the *total picture* you are trying to achieve. Will you be a happy person in your material/personal goals, while there are burning issues pushed conveniently under the mat?

Very often, we cannot make progress because there are underlying, unpleasant things in our lives which prevent us from moving at all. How can we start a journey if our car is stuck in deep snow? We have to do some shovelling first! Wishful thinking and distortion of the truth is not the remedy: you must work at the unpleasant goals too. If not, they'll be back to dampen your fireworks. As your aim is to draw up a complete picture, however, including a few more relevant goals should not disturb your calm. You now have the wherewithal to tackle all the issues of your life, consistently and positively.

So, to get what you want, you must make your list *comprehensive*. Sharpen that pencil again and prove you're an Open Person! How long is your goal list now? If the list has grown substantially because of these extra problem goals, it might be wise to do some weeding from the total. By carrying too many, you are apt to get bogged down. Your goals then receive less attention than they need. A total of 20–25 goals is heavy going. Try to aim for 15–18, and put the others in your pending file. Then from your final list, select key goals that underpin the whole picture, and work on them first.

THE SYSTEM IS FLEXIBLE

As a result of this review, there may perhaps be more goal possibilities for you to examine: you know best. You might want to solve a substantial problem quickly, with no grand plan for the future. For this, the same methods can be used, and as you gain familiarity and confidence in the procedures, you can improvise as you wish.

At this point you can see that almost any area of your life can be improved by conducting some methodical research, setting goals and finally applying the principles detailed in the previous chapter. You have no excuse for avoiding any goals! Not only can you declare any material and personal goals, but you can do some self-therapy as well. Your life-map is starting to look very comprehensive. It is all your own work – you should be really pleased with yourself.

REVIEW

1 You have the confidence to identify certain issues in your life which deserve attention.
2 You have written constructive goals to work on these issues.
3 Self-honesty and the acceptance of self have developed your self-esteem and integrity – you have become an Open Person.
4 You now know how to explore areas of higher development and reach a state of equilibrium with the world.

13   Success Isn't Too Easy

Nothing great was ever achieved without enthusiasm.

Ralph Waldo Emerson

OVERVIEW

Success is no more, and no less, than what we *make* it. Possessions, personal qualities, managing our lives – *we choose*. We must choose our *own* success – not that of popular craving.

Whatever our aspirations, we must remain true to the Open Person within. We must resolve to move *forward*, however short a pace. If we struggle with life, we are not in harmony with it, therefore accepting *what is* constitutes an element of success.

Personal achievement and growth demand work, but must be fun or the point is lost. Pursuing our aims will not be without doubts and backsliding, but we must learn to accept change and enjoy the journey. Nothing is impossible if we choose wisely and *believe* in what we are doing.

SUCCESS: ILLUSION OR ACHIEVEMENT?

Success has become larger than life through popular misconception. The very things we are commonly urged to aim for can be surprisingly hollow. In fact, success can be one of the shallowest pursuits on earth, if we have not understood its meaning with regard to our own lives. It may be nothing more than a fancy in our individual and collective minds: an illusion. True success, if we would but admit it, is learning to *discover and manage our own lives.*

You might take five steps forward in your personal growth goals, then be forced to take seven back. Learn to accept that five did indeed go forward, and you might see a way to take ten tomorrow, so that is success, just as much as owning a gleaming Porsche. Keep every avenue open. Every day, set out determined to move forward just a little more, no matter what side of the bed you got out of. And rejoice in any success, large or small. Be thankful and mindful of personal growth, as well as material results. You will always find it easier to fall back to your old ways. But you must resist this temptation, and consciously move away from the limiting and the negative.

FAILURES ACCOMPANY EFFORT, BUT SO DOES SUCCESS

You must expect to fail too, sometimes. That is reasonable, especially when we rely on our rational, conscious mind too much. When it happens, don't go to pieces and curse the universe! Learn to reflect on the positive benefits of the situation, rather than the bad news. For example, your home-based business might fail miserably, but the learning experience might groom you for a more interesting job. Strong people learn a great deal from mishaps and setbacks. Problems give us perspective and realism.

Recognize that if things don't go precisely their way, people are known to be impatient, very lazy and spiteful. That's human. So take care! Perhaps laziness is the single most persistent force of resistance to overcome. It is well known that personal growth requires work and attention. So apply the goal achievement methods honestly and with a co-operative spirit. Then go with the flow, in faith. And work hard. Success rarely 'just happens'; it has to be planned, *wanted* and worked for.

SUCCESS THROUGH ATTITUDE

Just getting through the average day successfully can be an exercise in pursuing success. What is a successful day? It is certainly not a day when you make everyone around you unhappy because you are complaining so much! Attitudes make the day go round. Try having more successful days!

Jack was on a long-distance business trip. The man beside him was an oil executive. When he got on, he complained that the aisle seat was taken. When he couldn't put his lap-top computer up in the rack, he argued furiously with the hostess over the safety regulations. The seat belt was twisted. He hated middle seats. He hated afternoon flights that were running late. And he particularly hated this airline's food.

At this point Jack gave up smiling and nodding blanket agreement. In conversation, he told the man he was a pilot. Somehow, they got onto the subject of water in aircraft fuel tanks. The man latched on immediately. Those stupid, irresponsible ground staff! Incompetent mechanics! Jack said it had happened to him once, and he had lost one engine for some minutes before a restart. Then the stranger asked if the big planes ran any risk. Jack nodded. His companion stayed quiet for some time.

Suddenly, the plane entered violent turbulence and the power was cut to flight idle. Through the noise and severe shaking, the intercom said something about fuel. There was a rapid descent with varied engine power. The man was rigid, pale, gripping the armrests.

Jack knew that the announcement was simply that they had a fuel stop at this airport, and also that the nearby mountains cause a choppy layer there in spring. The sudden descent was purely because they had a quick straight-in approach. However, he kept quiet.

On the next flight leg, the oil executive received all the snacks and refreshments with a smile. When they arrived at their destination, he turned sheepishly and said, 'I suppose you thought I was a bit hard on that flight attendant earlier, eh?'

Jack nodded in agreement.

Attitudes are important: they make your day and, ultimately, your life. Your attitude towards success should be balanced and positive: you may have your head in the clouds, but your feet should be firmly on the ground. Success is a frame of mind, and a feeling of achievement.

DON'T CHASE MERE IMAGES

A word of warning: if you can only see success as a large grey Rolls-Royce, a walled mansion and glamorous people lolling about being cool, think again. Words convey pictures, and should your picture of success be misleading to both levels of your consciousness, you can find yourself chasing the wrong rainbows. So be discerning and independent in choosing your type of success, instead of relying on whatever images society may provide. Start working towards success from *yourself outwards*.

Remember, too, your ideas on success are going to be different from those of the man or woman across the road. They may be working towards different goals entirely!

SUCCESS: YOUR DEFINITION

Ask a teenager what success is. Ask a child. Ask an elderly person. Ask some members of your peer group. Listen, say little and learn. You may compile a list including money, status, a career, possessions, a supportive partner, beautiful kids, contentment, happiness, good health, peace of mind and purpose, to name but a few. Older people tend to focus more on personal qualities, because their illusions about gathering possessions have largely faded. Younger people go for the trappings of life and the excitement. That's inevitable. I think wisdom plays its part, and also the relative maturity and level of personal growth of the individual, regardless of age.

So there are infinite definitions of success, but you alone have defined what success is for you. Now you must live with it, when it comes to you. Be ready, because it's not very far away! Your consciousness has been alerted; the wheels are in motion. You have learned how to access the most powerful tool that can help you: your own subconscious mind. You will soon see success slowly entering your life, just as you have pictured it!

DEFEATING DOUBT AND LOGIC, WELCOMING CHANGE

From personal experience, I know how difficult this journey is, and what can go wrong! So I have to both warn you and support you. Doubts will creep into your mind all the time. There will be a curious tension between the 'changing' person and the 'old' person. This may well cause you to feel physically drained at times, as energy is involved in the interchange between progress and resistance. Success is a difficult thing to achieve. Life itself is difficult! Did I ever say that change leading to success would be a breeze, free from stress and effort? I did say you've got what it takes...

Beware of thoughts such as: 'Success isn't for you, it's too difficult/you're not the successful type/you'll go strange with that meditation stuff/you'll lose all your friends.' That is just the conscious mind again, reasoning away, putting all the data into neat piles and showing you it doesn't add up. Remember, the subconscious mind is your guardian and protector. Keep in touch with it, for it will flush out the self-critical dialogue. Let your subconscious watch over you; feel secure that all is well, that you'll always cope. Keep your big picture in mind, every day.

STOP HERE AND THINK

Imagine yourself with your complete list of goals fulfilled. There you are, feeling particularly pleased with your perseverance and growth. But are you limiting yourself? Visualize ahead and consider:

- **Are you 'saving' yourself in any way?** Are you avoiding situations that would exercise some of your newly-acquired skills or qualities? If you wanted to overcome nervousness in public speaking and become a respected toastmaster, for example, how many speeches do you make each week?
- **Are you living up to your success by doing things consistently?** If one of your goals was to wear smarter, newer clothes, exploiting colours you never 'allowed' yourself before, are you still keeping your best outfits in the wardrobe? Why are you limiting yourself? Wear your new clothes successfully!
- **Do you give freely, of things and of time?** Are you clinging to all this success you created for yourself? People seldom want your money or your possessions, but what they value more than anything is your time. Spend time with those who need a gift of time.
- **Are you in love with yourself and all those around you?** Why not? Is your success conditional, patchy, reserved?
- **Are you allowing bad habits to creep back?** Do you smile at rain rather than scowl at it?
- **Have you closed your vision to certain things that are inconsistent with your picture of success?** If you consider beauty a measure of success, for instance, when you are out in public, do you only glance at the beautiful people? Find beauty in everyone: we are more than molecules and pretty faces, more than outward appearances.
- **Do you like money or are you in love with it?** By all means, attract money in great abundance, if that is your idea of success, but have you lost your awareness of what it is? Money is a gift, not a possession. Gifts pass from hand to hand. Use your money to spread your success, to give love and magic to another.
- **Are you a little embarrassed of your success?** Do you hide it from people to avoid their questions? (How did she do it? How can he drive a BMW now?) Are you pretending to be the same old person? There is no need to flaunt success, nor selfishly exploit it, but do not limit yourself either. Try to achieve a balance. Respect your new knowledge.

- **Have you extended your original boundaries of success, without developing further goals?** Do you think that now you've made it, everything must get bigger and grander? Don't play games with success or the processes you used to get there. You have a lifelong system here, not a fast horse that doubles your stake after the old blind pin trick!

RELATING TO YOUR OWN BIG PICTURE

Before you investigated the concepts of Open Persons, goals, change and focused thinking, you probably didn't know enough to get more from your life. Perhaps you believed you had reached your 'assigned' point of incompetence. Now you see possibilities you couldn't even contemplate back then. Do you think you have all the answers now? Be careful, for we never know all the answers. Retain a healthy pinch of humility.

Continue to help others. Little things are often enough. Hold the door open for someone, be courteous to a tourist, help someone in a wheelchair to negotiate a bad crossing. *Look for ways to help anyone and everyone.* Don't sneak off, telling yourself that some other fool will come along. Expect to be involved! Don't expect automatic gratitude – in fact, expect to be snubbed – but such behaviour can only add to your success. Think of it as a Universal Law. Give, and it all comes back multiplied. If you maintain this attitude, you will be *consistent with all people*, and be recognized as a person of integrity. That precious quality – integrity – will open doors for you in your career or business, in finance, leisure, relationships – in fact, in all your goals.

LIFE-PATHS ARE UNIQUE: YOURS, MINE

Why be jealous of others, when you can improve yourself and be successful in your own way? Don't copy or mimic the success of others. Their success is theirs. When you choose a pattern of success that suits *you*, it is even more wonderful.

An interesting exercise is to study the lives of great people: explorers, film directors, business leaders, politicians, great musicians, singers or actors. Such people often have the dream of success from childhood, but just as often may have realized their 'mission' in life after many fits and starts. Either way, the dream became their passion. It was their choice, completely. They kept it in their subconscious and worked towards it. Nothing ever stood in their way, *especially not them-*

selves. Very often, the backgrounds of great people were humble, under-privileged and difficult (adversity can be a rich source of 'desirable stress'; affluence can quell ambition). But their vision was alive, a deep, personal thing. You can learn from this.

QUALITY LIVING

Success is a quality of life that has many aspects to it. It can mean much more than money and flashy cars. Become the *person* you really *want to be* and enjoy a lovely car for what it is, no more. Nothing need deprive you of a possession you honestly desire in your life. But when flashy cars and images become the whole purpose of life, we must recognize the consequences of phoney substitutions: we become frustrated materialists and aimless hedonists. The 'total quality' of your life is vitally important. Mr Jones may have a 12-metre satellite dish on his lawn, but is all the television in the cosmos going to make him happy? Success is hard to pin down, isn't it?

THE CHOICE IS VERY MUCH UP TO YOU

Defining what you want is difficult. Setting goals that really mean something to you is difficult. Achieving those goals is difficult – but not *impossible.*

The truth is, the choices before you and the process of achieving your goals are moving targets. You must accept this and act accordingly. Stay open and aware. After some honest groundwork and silent meditation, the appropriate things for you will fall into place. Have faith that they will. You will enjoy your journey. You will have the right goals and the right success. Your life will be richer in every way. And the world will certainly be a much better place with you in it!

REVIEW

1 You have reviewed what you have learned and reconfirmed your ideas on success.
2 The negative forces of doubt, laziness and impatience have been recognized, but you know you will not be beaten by them.
3 Your personality and attitudes have become aligned with a successful approach to life, including common courtesies and making the world a better place.
4 You are satisfied with your choice of goals and feel that the 'success package' you are aiming for is right for you.

14   There Must Be More

Whoever believes that such inner activity can result only in vain imaginations is profoundly mistaken. Everything depends upon the manner in which it is undertaken, the goal which is aimed at, and the guidance (whether verbal, printed, or interior) which has been followed, as to what kind of result is obtained. The latter may certainly be as valueless as the mist to a traveller, but then it may also assume the highest value when the investigation is rightly conducted.

Paul Brunton

Do the very best you can; and then put up your old umbrella and keep the rain of criticism from running down the back of your neck.

Dale Carnegie

OVERVIEW

Life can only be the present and the future. Are we fully aware of the message for us in this statement? Opportunities are waiting to be picked, if only we can take control and focus on what we want!

Understanding the higher levels of the mind is our key to greatness.

Ideas on success, commitment, staying open and the power of the mind are revisited in this concluding chapter. We must now consolidate all that has been learned into the final touches to our life-map. Each one of us is a candidate for setting goals and implementing change, for learning to live the life we want. What else are we here for?

WHERE NOW?

We have studied together. You have had plenty to think about, significant exercises to consider and much soul-searching to grapple with. You have been coached in understanding the mind. You are now in possession of a set of tools you may not have possessed before. Your basic desire to be honest with yourself has helped you to this point. So what are you going to do about it?

LIFE IS TIME AND WHAT YOU DO WITH IT

An embarrassing question: how old are you? Be honest! Have you ever talked to actuaries or insurance people who deal in statistical life expectancy and pension terms? This is a worthwhile exercise; we should refresh our minds on mortality statistics every year, like a medical check-up! How many years do you think are available to you? It's such an odd, macabre topic that we treat it as a joke. But strolling through a cemetery in an unfamiliar town will bring it home. Take note of the ages of the deceased (quite a few forties and fifties, hmm?) What did the departed make of their lives, and what are you going to make of yours?

Life can only be the present and the future. The past is well and truly over. Two things are useless to a stricken pilot: the altitude above and the runway behind. When you're in a crisis, or merely thinking about one, the past is real enough, like the runway, but can you make use of it? The present need not be some sort of penance for the past.

Consider living your life as if you are leasing rather than owning it. When you rent a video player, do you forget about it, or do you watch as many films as possible over that wet weekend? The time with the machine and tapes is limited; see life the same way. Old people looking back on life often share regrets – regrets over the things they didn't do in life, not the things they did! If you don't make proper use of your life, you will eventually add remorse to your list of ills. Then panic. Fortunately, even panic has its good points. It can push you into doing something – like reading this type of book!

YOUR PRESENT, YOUR FUTURE, YOUR ATTITUDE

The present should be very real to you. Now is the time to apply all your senses and use what you have to greet the future. Of course, you are free to drop out at any point. But why not defy your laziness and see what's within your reach?

The future can be a magnificent unfolding of what you are struggling with at present. No matter what mess you are in or how deep your particular rut, there's hope! You have the answers inside you, although it's very easy to throw one's hands in the air and complain that whatever we are meant to be doing just isn't plain enough. Why aren't we given a sign? I'm sorry; it just isn't that simple. You won't find your life-map falling at your feet: you have to do your homework, and consult your subconscious. Our unique personalities, skills, talents, vocations, ambitions and goals are all within us. The task is to identify them, unlock them, set them free and use them. Quite simply, the signs are there, but make sure you are looking in the right places. If you've followed me this far, I'm sure you know where to look.

Stay open to all things or you will miss opportunities that are waiting to be taken. You might notice:

A chance to supply a new service or product.
A way to make your present family situation more active and interesting, thus more rewarding for you.
The chance of making new friends beyond your usual circle, who might be able to help you or share experiences with you.
Those persistent insights whispering: 'What you should be doing is seeing a bit of the world before settling down' or 'Don't panic, someone will appreciate your ideas and see your potential.'

Stop being judgemental. Are you perfect? Put all that judging energy into learning your goals and focusing on them. You can criticize others forever without changing anything; instead, get to work on your answers. Visualize, dream, paint the future in bright colours. A future in which you will be more magnificent. Is that such a frightening prospect?

Should you need to, review and revise your goals now, otherwise you might get out of focus. Also, remember that life is change, so be open to changing them.

DON'T GET HUNG UP ON FAILURE

You might think you're so lost, you'll never find yourself. But when you declare a problem, it's the first step towards the solution. Honesty with yourself, being an Open Person, is a precursor of the coming cure. There is no need to become depressed by your failings: reflect on them and plan to improve.

It is true that bad things happen to all people; life grants no exemptions. However, misfortune does not imply you are a failure. Identifying all bad experiences as failures, or as evidence that you are doomed to suffer, is a gross over-reaction. Learn to acknowledge successes, however small, and shake off gloomy thoughts about your failings. *You are what you think you are* in this regard, so think bright, positive thoughts, and focus on successful outcomes to all things.

GOALS ARE SET AT ALL POSSIBLE LEVELS

You already know that believing that goals only come in the Rolls Royce/swimming pool variety is ludicrous. You also know what you want, so have your own fun getting it, whether it's breeding champion chinchillas or writing children's books. Many people concentrate only on personal goals; they actually make a goal *not* to pursue material goals! Pursuing the elusive, predictable gravy train of personal comfort and affluence will never satisfy the discerning person. So choose wisely and individually. Then take your goals about with you everywhere – to the launderette, the board meeting, office, factory, church, football ground, ice rink, beach or bar; wherever you are.

UNDERSTANDING THE MIND

Understanding the mind is central to your progress. So it is worthwhile returning to the mind here, as a topic for review. If you have further questions, then consult books on psychology, psychotherapy or meditation, which specifically deal with the workings of the human mind. It is an unusual but intriguing interest. Please make the effort.

RECONSIDERING THE MIND

Remember that your *subconscious* mind is very much part of your total reality. It communicates in little whispers of meaning, rather than in words. We commonly call these 'intuition', 'creativity' or 'brainwaves'. Your conscious mind interprets the whispers, translating the details into words and images for you to work with. But don't always assume that the conscious mind has fully understood the message and passed it on correctly: it might be elaborating on it!

Sharing goals with your subconscious mind, and listening for instructions some time later, is really a process of *meaning*, rather than words. As you get to 'know' your goals, you will be able to transfer 'meaning' to your subconscious, not a string of words. While working in Norway, I studied children who could speak (and think) perfectly in two languages. Were their thoughts in Norwegian more clear to them than in English? They said no, but their parents believed thoughts in the native tongue were richer, more expressive. Would it be possible to create and witness identical thoughts in a Greek waiter and an Icelandic fisherman? Probably not, I concluded, but it really depends on the thoughts.

Communicated thoughts are subject to cultural and linguistic constraints (even within the same culture and language), although 'saying it another way' helps to clarify the construct. Since communication is such a complex process (words, tone, body language, etc.), we can only say that good approximations are possible. Sometimes (fortunately), words are not required to express meaning, and this is where we leave language, intellect and the conscious mind far behind.

Quite simply, there is a 'hierarchy of thought' and as you raise your level of consciousness, 'meaning' can be communicated more efficiently than by using our left-brain skills alone. Thinking becomes more of an art than a science. Perhaps you have seen it working: people are 'on the same wavelength', couples 'communicate without words' or a problem-solving team hits the solution 'as if they shared the same brain'. When you are 'talking' to your subconscious and communicating goals, words are first replaced by images, and they, in turn, by *pure meaning*. Think about it!

So try to reach the level of transferring 'meaning' to your subconscious as quickly as possible. Your subconscious mind will be impressed if you can communicate in this way. It will respond more efficiently. *Understanding the higher levels of the mind is your key to greatness.*

Jacqueline was sailing with friends in a 36-foot yacht. The weather was lovely and warm, with a good sailing breeze. The sails were trimmed perfectly. The wheel was light and easy. For some three or four minutes, they glided along in ideal conditions. Glenn Miller played from a cassette tape; the flag on the transom fluttered beautifully. They ate excellent sandwiches and sipped refreshing, cool beer. The only sounds came from the boat's motion and the music.

All at once, the group all stopped eating and sipping beer. In a collective moment, they stared at each other's faces, a quiet, common knowing in their eyes. A wonderful calm was upon them, an overwhelming sense of intense well-being. Words or mere thoughts had no meaning whatsoever at that instant.

When Jacqueline wrote about it later, she felt the energy of those glorious few seconds had been lost to communication altogether. Words can give a reasonable account of a small boat in pleasant waters, where the music of Glenn Miller and nice weather made five people feel good, but no more.

LIVE YOUR OWN LIFE

Once you realize you are more than molecules and conscious mind, you will begin to achieve more. Most people never get close to this realization. Consider yourself wise to seek out truth as you are doing.

Sadly, most people couldn't care less about who they are, or what real potential they have. And if people make no effort to investigate these things for themselves, then they have no option but to remain as they are. We are all responsible for our own lives, whatever political flag we fly, whatever philosophy makes sense to us. Who can breathe for you, think for you? Gathering excuses and blaming the system is fun for those who seek handy answers to tedious questions. But does that relieve you of ultimate responsibility for each hour of your day? If you won't open up and listen, the life you desire will pass you by. Through your actions thus far, you have joined the positive-thinking, self-help school of thought: you want to improve yourself and achieve something with your life. No doubt this book has strengthened your faith in yourself. I believe in you! You live your own life, *so why not sort it out and make something of it?*

TAKING CHARGE

People really can be in charge of their own lives, although rather than facing up to this exciting reality, we generally wait for circumstances and other people to define our lives. A job is lost: the world comes to an end. A relationship finishes: there are no alternatives. Brilliant ideas won't germinate: a dull life is all there is. This is the way many people live! They think it is easier to wait and see what falls from the sky than act to change the future. But of course this doesn't apply to you any more...does it?

No situation is hopeless, and nobody has a situation that cannot be improved. Each one of us is a candidate for setting goals and implementing change.

THE SYNERGY OF GROUPS

Just as each person can change the environment and circumstances they have control over, groups have a strong synergy to do the same.

Group progress is often stifled by the committee mentality. However, good things *are* happening; groups of dedicated people are 'getting there from here'.

Motivated groups achieve success through collective soul-searching, goal-setting and creative implementation. Although there might not be group 'deep silence and subconscious sessions', the successful leaders are certainly drawing on their subconscious energies to solve problems and achieve their goals.

Some examples might serve to highlight areas of transformation being achieved in this way. Inner city redevelopment projects around the world have shown how quite ordinary citizens have forged boldly ahead, against all the odds. Expanding community education has provided non-academic adult education, enabling 'late starters' to find new career and social paths. On a personal level, self-help groups have blossomed where professional help has been non-existent or slow to respond (in the areas of alternative medicine, effective parenting, group therapy, divorce and single parent support, meditation/relaxation and consciousness-raising, to name but a few). Similarly, self-improvement groups promote activities such as gaining confidence through public speaking, re-entry to the job market (mutual support groups), and all types of counselling.

At the multinational corporation level, the same methodology applies. Successful companies have recognized the role of people and innovative approaches in their organizations. The early scientific management models, quite austere in their treatment of humanity, have been largely replaced by more open systems of management. The rational, analytical, bean-counting model has had its day. Now we see employee participation in decisions at all levels, a drive for quality and customer service, and interest in the potential of each staff member, from the bottom to the top. Management development seminars are more likely to include meditation, left/right brain thinking, creative problem-solving and innovative visualization these days – a significant change from drooling over practice balance sheets and the wonders of information technology.

SELF-DEVELOPMENT IS A LIVING PROJECT

Whether alone, in a small self-help group or within a forward-thinking multinational, we can find people *consciously deciding to take a chance*. There is nothing to lose, after all, but the boredom from watching stagnation. Whether it concerns groups or individuals, the rules are the same. Just think what we could achieve in global terms if we all understood how to set and achieve individual goals which would benefit everyone! It has been said that it is easier to change the whole world than to change yourself: just a little more technology, better economic models, more exciting ideologies and more charismatic leadership, and we shall have a better world. But this is false! *Changing the world starts and ends with changing yourself.* You are in control of your unique, magnificent life experience. Improve on that, and then share it with the world.

THE BOTTOM LINE

The way to move is forward. You will never achieve the things you want for your life by clinging to the past. Are you unhappy, unfulfilled, uneasy with life as it is? So why must you go on like that? Have you decided that life is a punishment of some sort? Unpleasant things and setbacks hit us all, but don't waste the rest of your life analysing them. Learn from them; then move on to bigger and better things. You know how:

- Focus on the goals you have given such personal care to. Begin to live them now, as if they have arrived! Set your total mind to work and tap your inner resources.
- Change at a pace you can handle, and give some thought to those close to you. They might not be spinning at your speed.
- Stick with your inner resolve to *complete what you have started. Finishers* are achievers.
- Stop comparing yourself with others, above or below your station. Focus on yourself, but selflessly.
- Be honest with yourself and other people. Live in the moment and live it to the edges. Whatever you do is important, whether it's thrilling or mundane.
- Learn to laugh at yourself: you really can be funny!
- Be your own person, strong and resolute; refuse to be compromised or debased through some silly diversion or criticism. If you have good ideas about something, collect them and use them.
- Develop the facility of exchanging ideas with your subconscious mind. The power of the subconscious rivals the power of the atom, but of course this truth has seldom seen the light of day. Our growth as individuals, and as nations, depends on the increasing use of the subconscious mind.

- Trust your own ideas and feelings. Draw on what you have learned here and commit yourself to applying it. Your self-awareness has been expanded through these pages and through your own effort. Think of this self-awareness and learning as an 'inner support system'. No matter what you want from life, you now have a personalized system to initiate, plan and achieve your objectives.
- Stay open, whether it yields exciting work possibilities, healthier relationships or clearer understanding of others and the world we live in.

You can define the life you want and achieve it. What else are you here for? And why wait until it's too late? Never be too proud or scared to try. Consciously vote to enjoy life. See the possibilities and move towards them. You alone are in command of your choices, your destiny; you are free, always. There must be more than you allowed yourself in the past. Now is the time to find it.

I have walked some way with you. I hope your map is almost complete now. It takes courage to continue on this journey, but you have already left the crossroads quite a way behind. Look back on where we have been. You have passed a few interesting milestones along the way, haven't you? Pause for a moment to congratulate yourself. You deserve it. Take with you the things you have learned here, and what you have learned about yourself through the exercises and soul-searching. Now, make your decision to proceed, to re-create yourself. I wish you every success with all your goals. Have a rewarding, happy life!

REVIEW

1 You have reviewed and consolidated what you have learned.
2 The act of commitment has given you the essential energy to focus on your goals and achieve them.
3 You know that your subconscious mind will continue to seek out opportunities on your behalf.
4 You welcome the responsibility you feel for your own life.
5 You have learned to trust your 'inner support system' and have gained confidence in everything you do.

Recommended Reading

Abercrombie, M.L.J., *The Anatomy of Judgement* (Pelican, London, 1960).

Argyle, Michael, *The Psychology of Interpersonal Behaviour* (Penguin, Harmondsworth, 1983).

Assagioli, Roberto, *Psychosynthesis* (Turnstone Press, Wellingborough, 1975).

——, *The Act of Will* (The Aquarian Press, Wellingborough, 1990).

Baddeley, Alan, *The Psychology of Memory* (Harper & Row, New York and London, 1976).

Berne, Eric, *Games People Play* (Penguin, Harmondsworth, 1968).

Bolles, Richard, *The Three Boxes of Life and How to Get Out of Them* (Ten Speed Press, Berkeley, California, 1978).

——, *What Color Is Your Parachute?* (Ten Speed Press, Berkeley, California, 1982).

Brunton, Dr Paul, *The Inner Reality* (Hutchinson, London, 1970).

Carnegie, Dale, *How to Stop Worrying and Start Living* (Simon & Schuster, New York, 1985).

——, *How to Win Friends and Influence People* (Cedar Books, London, 1988).

De Bono, Edward, *Lateral Thinking* (Pelican, London, 1977).

——, *The Happiness Purpose* (Pelican, London, 1979).

Frankl, Victor E., *Man's Search for Meaning* (Simon & Schuster, New York, 1967).

Goffman, E., *The Presentation of Self in Everyday Life* (Pelican, London, 1972).

Handy, Charles, *The Future of Work* (Basil Blackwell, London, 1985).

Hill, Napoleon, *Think and Grow Rich* (Thorsons, Wellingborough, 1984).

Janov, Dr Arthur, *The Primal Scream* (Sphere Books, London, 1973).

Jung, Carl G., *Memories, Dreams, Reflections* (Fontana, London, 1983).

Kübler-Ross, Elisabeth, *On Death and Dying* (Macmillan, New York, 1964).

Kushner, Harold S., *When Bad Things Happen to Good People* (Schocken Books, New York, 1981).

Laing, R.D., *The Divided Self* (Pelican, London, 1965).

——, *Self and Others* (Pelican, London, 1971).

LeShan, Lawrence, *How to Meditate: A Guide to Self-Discovery* (Thorsons, Wellingborough, 1988).

Mackenzie, R. Alec, *The Time Trap* (McGraw-Hill, New York, 1975).

Markham, Ursula, *Self-Hypnosis* (Thorsons, Wellingborough, 1988).

Maslow, Abraham H., *Motivation and Personality* (Harper & Brothers, New York, 1954).

McLuhan, Marshall, *Understanding Media* (McGraw-Hill, New York, 1965).

Morris, Desmond, *Manwatching* (Jonathan Cape, London, 1977).

Nolan, Vincent, *The Innovator's Handbook* (Sphere Books, London, 1987).

Norwood, Robin, *Women Who Love Too Much* (Arrow Books, London, 1986).

Peale, Norman Vincent, *The Power of Positive Thinking* (Prentice-Hall, New York, 1956).

Peck, Dr M. Scott, *The Road Less Traveled* (Simon & Schuster, New York, 1978).

Peters, T.J. and Waterman, R.H., *In Search of Excellence* (Harper & Row, New York, 1982).

Powell, John, *Why Am I Afraid to Tell You Who I Am?* (Fontana, London, 1975).

Rogers, Carl, *On Becoming a Person* (Houghton Mifflin, Boston, 1961).

Russell, Peter, *The Brain Book* (Routledge & Kegan Paul, London, 1979).

Samuels, Mike and Nancy, *Seeing with the Mind's Eye* (Random House, New York, 1976).

Selye, Hans, *The Stress of Life* (McGraw-Hill, New York, 1956).

——, *Stress Without Distress* (Corgi, London, 1987).

Sheehy, Gail, *Passages: Predictable Crises of Adult Life* (Bantam, New York, 1977).

Shone, Ronald, *Creative Visualization* (Thorsons, Wellingborough, 1984).

Shrout, R.N., *Self-Improvement Through Self-Hypnosis* (Thorsons, Wellingborough, 1987).

Toffler, Alvin, *Future Shock* (Pan, London, 1971).

Of further interest . . .

KNOWING WHEN TO QUIT

HOW TO STOP FIGHTING BATTLES AND GET ON WITH YOUR LIFE

Jack Barranger

If you are stuck in a rut one of the hardest things to do is to get out of it. After all there are a million reasons for staying in a boring job, a dead-end relationship, an environment you hate, or any situation that doesn't provide what you really want . . . or are there?

Jack Barranger's inspiring book will show you that it is simply not true that 'winners never quit'. If you are in a depressing, stifling situation you may be suffering from 'the staying syndrome', holding on to the status quo rather than striking out for what you deserve.

This book will provide you with the tools for escape. It is a complete decision-making kit that will help you analyse your reasons for staying, your need to leave, how your decision will affect others, how to deal with people who try to give you advice, and when to make crucial moves towards a positive new life.

The key to change is to ask yourself the right questions. *Knowing When to Quit* will show you how to do just that, and you will be amazed at how clear your path becomes.

WHAT TO SAY WHEN YOU TALK TO YOURSELF

Powerful *New* Techniques to Programme
Your Potential for Success!

SHAD HELMSTETTER

You don't have to be crazy to talk to yourself!

We all talk to ourselves all of the time, usually without realizing it. And most of what we tell ourselves is negative, counterproductive and damaging . . . preventing us from enjoying a fulfilled and successful life.

Shad Helmstetter's simple but profound techniques, based on an understanding of the processes of the human brain, have enabled thousands of people to get back in control of their lives.

By learning how to talk to yourself in new ways, you will notice a dramatic improvement in all areas of your life. You will feel better and accomplish more. It will help you achieve more at work and at home, lose weight, overcome fears, stop smoking and become more confident. And it works.

Shad Helmstetter, Ph.D., is a bestselling author of many personal growth books, and the leading authority in the field of Self-Talk.